DIALOGUES AT ONE INCH ABOVE THE GROUND

NANZAN STUDIES IN RELIGION AND CULTURE
James W. Heisig, General Editor

Heinrich Dumoulin. *Zen Buddhism: A History. Vol. 1, India and China. Vol. 2, Japan.* Trans. James Heisig and Paul Knitter (New York: Macmillan, 1988, 1989, 1994)

Frederick Franck, ed. *The Buddha Eye: An Anthology of the Kyoto School* (New York: Crossroad, 1982)

Frederick Franck. *To Be Human Against All Odds* (Berkeley: Asian Humanities Press, 1991)

Winston L. King. *Death Was His Kōan: The Samurai-Zen of Suzuki Shōsan* (Berkeley: Asian Humanities Press, 1986)

Paul Mommaers and Jan Van Bragt. *Mysticism Buddhist and Christian: Encounters with Jan van Ruusbroec* (New York: Crossroad, 1995)

Robert E. Morrell. *Early Kamakura Buddhism: A Minority Report* (Berkeley: Asian Humanities Press, 1987)

Nagao Gadjin. *The Foundational Standpoint of Mādhyamika Philosophy.* Trans. John Keenan (New York: SUNY Press, 1989)

Nishida Kitarō. *Intuition and Reflection in Self-Consciousness.* Trans. Valdo Viglielmo et al. (New York: SUNY Press, 1987)

Nishitani Keiji. *Nishida Kitarō* (Berkeley: University of California Press, 1991)

Nishitani Keiji. *Religion and Nothingness.* Trans. Jan Van Bragt (Berkeley: University of California Press, 1985)

Nishitani Keiji. *The Self-Overcoming of Nihilism.* Trans. Graham Parkes and Setsuko Aihara (New York: SUNY Press, 1990)

Paul L. Swanson. *Foundations of T'ien-T'ai Philosophy: The Flowering of the Two-Truths Theory in Chinese Buddhism* (Berkeley: Asian Humanities Press, 1989)

Takeuchi Yoshinori. *The Heart of Buddhism: In Search of the Timeless Spirit of Primitive Buddhism.* Trans. James Heisig (New York: Crossroad, 1983)

Tanabe Hajime. *Philosophy as Metanoetics.* Trans. Takeuchi Yoshinori et al. (Berkeley: University of California Press, 1987)

Taitetsu Unno, ed. *The Religious Philosophy of Nishitani Keiji: Encounter with Emptiness* (Berkeley: Asian Humanities Press, 1990)

Taitetsu Unno and James Heisig, eds. *The Religious Philosophy of Tanabe Hajime: The Metanoetic Imperative* (Berkeley: Asian Humanities Press, 1990)

Hans Waldenfels. *Absolute Nothingness: Foundations for a Buddhist-Christian Dialogue.* Trans. James Heisig (New York: Paulist Press, 1980)

Dialogues at one inch above the ground

**RECLAMATIONS OF BELIEF
IN AN INTERRELIGIOUS AGE**

James W. Heisig

A Herder & Herder Book
The Crossroad Publishing Company
New York

The Crossroad Publishing Company
www.crossroadpublishing.com

Printed in the United States of America

The typesetting for this book was done by the Nanzan Institute for Religion
and Culture, Nagoya, Japan.

Library of Congress Cataloging-in-Publication Data
Heisig, James W., 1944–
Dialogues at one inch above the ground : Reclamations of belief in an
    interreligious age / James W. Heisig.
    p. ; cm.
    Includes bibliographical references.
    ISBN 0-8245-2114-5 (alk. paper)
        1. Buddhism. 2. Buddhism — Relations — Christianity. 3. Chris-
        tianity and other religions — Buddhism. I. Title.
    BQ4012. H45 2002
    294.3'32—dc21   2003001246

1 2 3 4 5 6 7 8 9 10 06 05 04 03

ISBN 978-0-8245-2114-1 (paperback)

Contents

Contents

Introduction

EACH OF THE ESSAYS in this book addresses a particular aspect of the dialogue with the spirituality of our times. Behind them stands the simple conviction that much of the faith of traditional religion has shifted to the secular realm, and that neither traditional religion nor the saeculum has adjusted to the situation. Both are suffering from the dislocation.

I find it hard to rush to the conclusion that ours is simply an age of disbelief, that the saeculum has out and out lost its fundamental faith—whether in the world we can see or in the world we cannot—and that organized religion has allowed the pressures of survival in a globalized economy to drain its soul of faith in the things that matter. It is rather that we are no longer able to pillar many of the beliefs and symbols we have received from the past in the places we were raised to do. The questions this poses reach deeper than individual egoism or the failure to measure up to convictions. They point to disbelief in the very ideas and institutions that faith is supposed to enthuse.

In the attempt to distinguish between what we believe and what we have been made to believe, and at the same time to accept responsibility for what the ideas and institutions we inherited have done to us, we end up disoriented. With no place to go and no place to stay at home, we sail an uncertain course, persuaded at one moment by our insight into what has gone wrong, confused at the next by which alternatives to pursue. That so many of those adrift in these waters but driven by the will to believe *something* should choose to beach their reason and morality on one of the available islands of certitude, religious or otherwise, is hardly to be wondered at.

At a time of the dislocation of belief, perhaps it is the will to disbelieve that is the greater virtue. Simple skepticism aimed at the doctrines and institutions that have failed to provide a ground for the faith and hope and love of the age, however reasonable or morally inspired, is not enough. Disbelief must be deepened and cultivated if it is ever to point the way to relocating faith in new doctrines and institutions. Like the angel caught in Jacob's grip at Penuel, it must be wrestled with until it delivers a blessing we can pass on to those that follow us. This book is the record of my own attempts to dialogue with the kind of disbelief that I believe that faith at the onset of the twenty-first century obliges us to.

The nine essays that make up the collection deal directly with religious themes, all of them taken up from a Christian point of view and all of them written in Japan, where I have spent the past quarter century engaged in research on religion and philosophy, East and West. A brief note has been appended to each explaining the context of its composition.

In reading over the essays, all written during the last decade of the twentieth century, I am struck by a thread of naivete that runs through them. Although simplicity of argument may not be endearing to those who expect a more studied response to the problems taken up here, I find it helpful when it comes to clearing up my mind on matters of importance. Personally, these dialogues with the dislocation of belief have also provided some refreshment from the usual pace of academic research, not to mention some reprieve from the accompanying pressures of avoiding error at all costs. In this regard, I am a little disturbed to find myself today in such substantial agreement with so much of what I have written, and have to ask myself if there are not things I have overlooked along the way, momentous things that others might notice better in the rash and simple statement than in the guarded aside slipped unobtrusively into more professional writing. I would be disappointed if this were not the case, and it would frustrate one of the main motives for republishing the pieces in this form.

It is said of the twelfth-century Buddhist poet Saigyō that he tried to live at "one inch above the ground." This seems to me just the right posture for dialoguing with the spiritual side of disbelief: not with one's two feet planted firmly in the everyday, not walking on the clouds—but floating a thumb's length above the ground. John the evangelist advises us to "be in the world but not of the world." I like to think that in dialogues with other spiritual ways, secular or religious, it is possible to be *of* my Christian tradition without standing *in* it. If religions are to coexist with one another and with the saeculum, and to maintain their faith in one another, this posture has to be more than an intellectual exercise entrusted to specialists trained in "dialogue." It has to be cultivated as a new virtue for which nothing in tradition gives us old habits to rely on.

9 August 2001
Rio de Janeiro

Sufficiency and Satisfaction

Recovering an Ancient Symbolon

In 1990 an International Zen Symposium was convened in Kyoto on the theme "Religion and Ethics in the Modern World." As the last of the invited guests to speak, I tried to think through a moral equivalent of Leibnitz's principle of sufficient reason. The immediate aim of what I there called the "principle of sufficiency" was not to explain the world but to guide the way we consume it: to locate morally acceptable limits to the acquisition of goods and services, and to rescue the assessment of needs from its current status as one more object of consumption.

During the course of the week, we had taken an excursion to the Ryōan-ji temple, home of Japan's most famous rock garden. Although not my first visit, I was struck by the inscription on a small stone basin in an inconspicuous corner of the temple grounds: "All I need to know is how much is enough."

It was as if that small basin had been resting on the native earth of Japan for nearly three centuries, waiting with mystic patience as feudalistic society made way for industrialization and market-economies, as technological innovations and information-intensive business began to challenge the supremacy of national interests, as the accumulation of wealth created an appetite for consumption that would imperil the survival of civilized life—waiting for the time to come when its simple truth might be lifted up from the stone and out of the tranquility of its surroundings into the buzzing confusion of the marketplace.

My original paper had ended with the admission that I

5

> could not see any way out of the economic bind that holds
> the contemporary imagination captive. That evening I sat
> down and rewrote the conclusion in the light of that simple
> inscription. Later I pursued the history of the inscription
> and landed eventually in an untranslated third-century
> Chinese sūtra, which became the subject of the following
> essay.

First published in *Studies in Formative Spirituality* 14/1 (1993): 55–74. Reprinted in *Dialogue* 21 (1994): 69–90.

SOME YEARS AGO I argued for the introduction of a "principle of sufficiency" into economic theory and consumer ethics.[1] My guiding image was a cryptic saying carved into a *tsukubai*, or stone water basin, at Ryōan-ji in Kyoto: 吾唯足知 All I know is how much is enough. It seemed to me, and still does, that knowing how much is enough is a useful, if badly neglected, skill. The general depletion of the planet's resources, the systematic promotion of poverty, and the growing addiction to surplus call for a new way of looking at the activities of exchanging goods and services. The *tsukubai* was simply a convenient place in the past from which to have a second look at where we have landed ourselves in the present.

Stone basins became a standard fixture in the Japanese tea garden from the early sixteenth century. They were typically set at the entrance to a tea house as a place for people to cleanse their hands in preparation for the tea ceremony. The name *tsukubai* (蹲踞 = crouching) comes from the fact that one had to bend the body over deeply to perform the ablution. The round stone basin at Ryōan-ji—a temple known throughout the world for its enigmatic fifteenth-century rock garden—dates from the end of the seventeenth century. The origins of the actual saying, which is arranged clockwise around a hollowed out square through which water is drawn, are obscure; but the influence of Chinese Buddhism, as we shall see, is unmistakable.

I confess I was annoyed by the English translation that the keepers of the temple had settled on: *I just know how to be contented.*[2] The idea of mere contentment seemed undeserving of the religious surroundings, of the tea ceremony and of the suggestive-

7

ness of the Chinese characters themselves. At the same time, the two characters which I preferred to read "knowing how much is enough" *do* also mean "being satisfied." It is as if the principle of sufficiency and the art of satisfaction were intended to form the two halves of a *sym-bolon,* a *coincidentia oppositorum* suggested by the squaring of the circle in the design of the basin. It is to recover this connection that I return to the *tsukubai* for yet another look.

If there is one ingredient in human spirituality that qualifies as truly universal, it is the quest for satisfaction. It runs through history like a bright red thread on which every pearl of culture and language and religious belief, the bright and the dull, the noble and the ignoble, can be strung in single array. But precisely because the quest for satisfaction is so ubiquitous a feature of human life, there can be no final consensus about what it means to be satisfied. The very idea of feeling "full" is in constant flux from one stage in life to the next, from one age to the next. What is more, the quest of one satisfaction almost always obliges us to dispense with the quest of others; and no satisfaction is ever quite enough to quench the thirst for still more. In a word, the pursuit of satisfaction always requires concrete insight into just how much is enough. This is the bedrock of what we now call spirituality. It is also solid ground from which persons raised in the Christian tradition can contemplate the rich inheritance of the Buddhist tradition.

In our own day, dialogue between Buddhism and Christianity has given fresh importance to the search for universal patterns of thought, experience, and imagery, for consensus about what it means to be homo religiosus. At the same time, the difficulty of encounter with religions considered "primitive" or "closed" to dialogue shows again and again how very culturally bound are the standards by which we decide that some idea or practice deserves the label of "universally human." Meantime, the continued loosening of the hold of state and religion over individual conscience has opened the floodgates to a proliferation of neutral, non-aligned, global organizations aimed at monitoring the uniform moral progress of the human community, all too often blissfully unaware of the elective principles they are inflicting on others as inalienable truths. And yet, for all its risks and pitfalls, the conversion of interest away from sectarian religion and ethics towards a spirituality grounded in the universal principles marks a watershed in modern religious awareness. It is also the starting point for the transition from the *enforcement of common principles* to the *discipline of common virtues*. This is the wider background against which I wish to consider the relationship between the pursuit of satisfaction and the principle of sufficiency.

The interlocking ideas of needs and sufficiency have their roots in bodily satisfaction, and as such lie close to the origins of language and consciousness. Disciplining them to a spiritual purpose, however, requires corresponding shadow-ideas of greed and surfeit. What the modern economic imagination has done to the notions of *sufficiency* and *needs* in the process of translating them into *supply* and *demand* is, in effect, to erase that shadow. But without awareness of greed and surfeit, the pursuit of satisfying needs is neither bodily nor spiritually human.

Despite lexical and etymological similarities, the paired terms *sufficiency-needs* and *supply-demand* have come to carry almost opposite meanings for us. We have no trouble understanding ideas like "increasing supply to meet the current demand" and "stimulating demand to dispose of the current supply." To an age or culture that lacks such a predisposition, such phrases cannot but sound brutal, unjust, at best nonsensical. One need only transpose the terms to appreciate the effect: the idea of "satisfying needs by adjusting the perception of what is sufficient" or "generating needs in order to justify the sufficiency of current production" sound like strategies for poverty and waste.

The transposition is not entirely fair, but it does give some sense of how habits of language can determine what is worth thinking about and what not. Take the ideas of greed and surfeit, for instance. Although the words still make perfect sense to us, they are all but outlawed in the marketplace of economic polity, relegated to the status of "private affairs of conscience." In other words, it is only through a systematic dislocation of common sense that the modern economic imagination is able to function without a spirituality. Small wonder, as Jacques Ellul has pointed out, that the history of technology and the history of propaganda have evolved together.

The dislocation of spirituality would not have been possible without the invention of the modern "individual" and its accompanying distinction between the everyday ego and a truer, deeper Self. Current ruling metaphors of the Self have given new meaning to the idea of satisfaction and fulfillment, of completion, of being "filled up" and "made whole." The condition that one is saved from is one of "emptiness" or "dividedness." Such talk, as well as the transfer of talk of greed and surfeit from the social to the private sphere, would be meaningless without the modern notion of a reified Self. This is a question to which I hope to return at a later date.[3] For now it is enough to note that the goal of self-satisfaction, whatever its limitations, has also given the modern individual a place from which to negotiate a stance in religious pluralism.

Writing at the beginning of the twentieth century, William James captured the mood that remains with us still: "The warring gods and formulas of the various religions do indeed cancel each other, but there is a certain uniform deliverance in which religions all appear to meet."[4] For James, this uniform deliverance lay in the idea of healing a wound, easing an uneasiness—in short, salvation. Ideas of salvation in the world's religions, he saw, all rely on the metaphor of release from the suspense of dissatisfaction, from the pressure of desires physical and mental, high and low, which mark our lives at every turn. (Artificially embraced dissatisfactions may have therapeutic value for those who can afford the luxury of an environment where dissatisfactions are not otherwise thrown up in abundance. For such individuals, the overdose may even be enlightening, but often enough the asceticism is no more than a spiritual aberration.)

Reconnecting the symbolon of satisfaction and sufficiency is simple enough for the individual in the abstract. What is harder is the creation of a supporting context in time and space. Such contexts are largely absent in current institutions that we participate in as members of society, as well as in our patterns of consuming goods and services. One of the reasons we turn to scriptures, and why we call them "sacred," is that they liberate the imagination from the captivity of those institutions and patterns. A scripture is *holy* only for the individual with the discipline to listen to it; it becomes *saving* only when one exercises the virtues of conviviality.

The discipline of listening to a text is a fragile enterprise, especially in an age that has become accustomed to the manipulation of print as ours has become. There is no need to argue for the superior wisdom of ancient texts over contemporary ones in order to know the emancipation that can come from losing oneself in the sacred territories of the arcane and slightly exotic. In the pages that follow I would like to consider the symbolon of sufficiency and satisfaction in a Buddhist text I have come to consider sacred, the *Sūtra of the Buddha's Final Instruction*.[5]

It is hardly surprising that scholars should have had trouble classifying the sūtra as either "Hīnayāna" or "Mahāyāna," so universal and nonsectarian is its appeal. The instructions are neither deeply philosophical nor in any sense entangled in apologetics. The careful interweaving of imagery and ideas suggests that the whole was intended to be read as a meditation rather than as a catechism, and this is how I have chosen to translate it. The text that we have appears to be an early fifth-century translation by Kumārajīva for which no original Sanskrit or Tibetan versions remain. There are many similarities to the legendary biography of the Buddha, the *Buddhacarita*,[6] composed by the second-century Sanskrit poet Aśvaghoṣa, and to the early collections of aphorisms known as the *Dhammapada*.[7] I shall note a few of them in passing.

The Chinese is elegant and flowing, as befits the occasion of the Buddha's last words before passing away. It was a popular text in classical China and in Japan, especially in Zen, where it is recognized as one of the "Three Sūtras of the Founder."

The italics in the translation were added to make it easier for the reader to move forwards and backwards through a text fragmented by my running commentary. Further, in translating a sūtra that has so much to say about the dangers of taking license and the importance of clearing the mind, I felt the need for keeping some check on my work without at the same time cluttering the text. The footnotes provided a convenient receptacle for this purpose and should not be mistaken for proof of adequate research.

THE DISCIPLINE OF VIRTUE

In the still of the night, the Buddha lies under a tree dying. He turns to the disciples there with him and lays out the heart of his teaching in brief and simple terms. He begins by praising the holy rule of the monk:

> My dear monks, after I have gone see that you treasure the rule of the life you have chosen, for it will be your deliverance. Cherish it like a light met in the darkness, like a fortune come to a beggar. *Make the rule your master and learn from it well.* I would teach you no differently if I were to remain behind in the world.

> You who keep the rule in its purity, do not traffic in buying and selling; have no home and lands of your own; neither are you to keep tenants or servants, or to breed animals. Avoid all seeding and planting and accumulation of wealth as if they were afflictions. Reaping and mowing, tilling the soil, digging the earth, taking medicinal cures, seeking the advice of the fortune-tellers, trusting in those who read one's fate in the stars, divine one's luck from the phases of the moon, or calculate the number of one's days—all these things are *unsuited to the life you have chosen.*

In counseling his followers to live up to their choices, the Buddha does not pronounce on the inherent value of any activity proscribed by the rule. He asks them only to discipline themselves in the virtues that best respond to what they seek from life and to reject anything that weakens their resolve. The dictates of the rule are not grounded in abstract principles that need rational defense, but in the concrete immediacy of a drive for something deeper than current social conventions. Only by detaching oneself from the activities that feed conventional truth can one cultivate a mind clear enough and pure enough to *see through* what is wanting in the ruling modes of thought:

> Be moderate, eat regularly, make a clean living. Do not take part in worldly affairs or government diplomacy, keep away from sorcery and elixirs, do not curry favor with nobility, avoid excessive informality and familiarity. To leave all these things behind, you will need to keep a pure heart and a clear mind. Do not bother trying to keep your faults and failures hidden. Do not feign eccentricity or charm. When people offer you food and drink or clothing or bedding or medicine, look at the amount and consider how much is enough. Take just what you need and do not pile up a surplus.

The two Chinese characters that carry the injunction to "consider how much is enough" 足知 are what I have called the *principle of sufficiency*. As noted above, the Buddha is not heralding a concept but a virtue, a capacity for insight whose truth lies in its exercise. Thus, although these same glyphs are also used to render the Sanskrit terms *tuṣṭi* (complete knowledge) and *saṃtuṣṭa* (feeling satisfied), the literary pedigree here is distinctively Chinese. The double-entendre does not play merely on a grammatical reversal of the word *knowing* 知 but on the ambiguity of the character 足, which can mean both sufficiency and satisfaction. Two passages in the *Lao-tzu (Tao-te ching)* bring this double meaning out clearly:

> To know when you have enough is to be rich. (ch. 33)

> If you store much away, you're bound to lose a great deal.
> Therefore, if you know contentment, you'll not be disgraced. (ch. 44)[8]

The English translator has had to chose contrasting meanings based on the context. The Chinese reader does not—they are *both* present at the same time. Later I will return to this matter. For now, it is enough to notice the entailment of one in the other, and that this is apparently something the Chinese has added to the original text.

The same thing can be seen in the following lines from the *Dhammapada,* the Chinese translation of which recapitulates the content of the sūtra we are considering here:

> The greatest benefit is to be free of illness.
> The greatest wealth is to know how much is enough.
> The greatest friend is the ability to see clearly.
> The greatest pleasure is to step out of the mire of convention.[9]

The second line in the corresponding Pali text translates into English as "Contentment is the highest wealth." Here, *santuṭṭhi* is rendered as contentment, whereas the Chinese also suggests the sense of "knowing how much is enough."[10] The final phrase is normally translated—even in Japanese versions—as "attaining nirvana." I have kept a more literal rendition of the two characters transliterating the word *nirvāṇa* in order to draw attention to the interpretation that the Chinese adds to the transliteration: the glyph for *mud* is also used as a verb to express being *mired* in social convention, old ways of thinking.[11] The continuation of the Buddha's instruction brings us to the same point:

> This, in a word, is what it means to keep the rule. It is through the rule that obedience will set you free. That is why it is called "the deliverance." Rely on the rule and it will bring you to the concentration and wisdom that extinguishes the cause of suffering. Be faithful to the rule, dear monks, and do not violate it. One who lives the rule participates in the goodness of the Dharma. No goodness or virtue can come to one who takes the rule but does not keep it. Know this well: *the rule is the primary abode of tranquility and virtue.*

The text likens the rule to a home-away-from-home for those who have left house and home and social convention to seek truth. The idea of discipline advanced here as a "freeing obedience" entails both learning from the rule and becoming its master.

From here on the text focuses on the latter, beginning with the reappropriation of the body from selfishness, routine, and social custom.

My dear monks, once you have made yourself properly at home in the rule, you must set to regaining control of your senses. This means not letting yourself be led around by what you can see and hear and smell and taste and touch, like the herdsman who raises his staff to keep his animals from straying into other people's crops. *Giving license to the senses prevents you from setting limits.* It puts you on an ill-tempered horse without a bridle. Sooner or later it will throw you into a ditch.

The control of the senses being taught here has little in common with the negative assessment of the body that has plagued Christian and Buddhist spiritualities alike. Here it is not a low esteem of the body but a sense of awe for the workings of the mind that is primary. The image of the senses as a horse run wild or a band of thieves makes sense only when we understand what has happened as a result: the mind can no longer see clearly.

When a thief robs you of your possessions, the suffering only lasts as long as you live. *When the senses rob you, the injury lives on and on.* The effect is immense. So take care. The wise person does not sit idly by but takes control of the senses. Think of them like a band of thieves on the loose and arrest them. Even if you indulge them, they will wear down in no time anyway.

The control of the senses is not aimed at the repression of an evil but at the reappropriation of what has been stolen. The point is to reclaim a clarity of mind that has been expropriated by the distraction of the senses. It is not a flight from pleasure—not even from sensual pleasure—but a dread of the damage that ignorance can work. More than things that deprive the senses one should fear the things that can muddy the spirit, as the continuation of the passage states:

The master of the senses is the mind, which is why you must all keep good control of the mind. Poisonous snakes, wild beasts, treacherous brigands, ravaging fires—none of these are as frightening as a mind gone out of control. It is like someone holding a jar of fresh honey and feeling so excited that he does not even notice the deep hole underfoot. Or it is like a monkey running from a rogue elephant on the loose and just making it safely to a nearby tree. It jumps about wildly, unable to contain itself for joy. Dispose of such a mind quickly before it yields to license and disregards the good of others. *The mind out of control cannot gather itself together and exert its best effort.* So work hard, dear monks, be diligent of spirit, and bring your mind to submission.

Without the ability to see clearly, the Buddha tells his followers, the mind is the mere plaything of the senses. When consumption of the sensual world—the sights and sounds, the smells and tastes and touches—reaches the point of greed or gluttony, the ill effects are both moral and physical. Only insight can heal sensuality and see through particular addictions to the underlying addiction to addiction. This is the point of the critique of the expropriation of mind by sensual *license.*

The dying Buddha turns to a discussion of reappropriating the senses by turning to the matter of physical needs:

My dear monks, think of food and drink as if they were medicine. *Whether you like the taste or not should have nothing to do with how much or how little you consume.* Take just enough to sustain yourself and to ward off hunger and thirst. Be like the bee who takes the flavor of the flower but leaves the color and the fragrance untouched. Accept the offerings that the faithful make to you and use them to fend your ills. Do not ask for too much, lest you test their good will to the breaking point. The wise farmer knows how to calculate the strength of an ox and not to make it exert itself beyond its limits.

At this point the text speaks only of the importance of restraint, with no attempt to explain the reason why it should matter. The oversight appears to be deliberate. The silence has the effect of suggesting a coming apology for monastic asceticism. In fact, as we shall see, this is not at all the case. But first, the Buddha speaks of the dangers of sleep and the virtue of shame:

> The daytime is for exerting the mind and cultivating the practice of what is true and good. Do not waste it. Nor should you squander the first and last watches of the night. See yourself through the middle watch by reciting the scriptures. *Things that induce sleep make the course of a life empty and futile.* Never lose sight of the fact that the world is always burning in the flames of impermanence. Seek your deliverance straightaway—*do not fall asleep!*

> The passions of the mind are ever lying in wait, with a murderous vengeance beyond compare. Suddenly you awaken with a start. Why? Because the passions lie coiled in your breast like a poison serpent. There is a black viper asleep in your room. Use the rule like an iron hook to drive it away. Once the serpent is outside, then you can sleep in peace. To fall asleep with it there is shameless. *Wear your shame with honor.* Let it be your iron hook when you fail the rule. Always feel your shame, my dear monks. Do not displace it but let it linger for a while. Withdraw from its disgrace and you lose all virtue. *One who knows shame abides in the goodness of the Dharma.* One who does not is no different from the birds and the beasts.

With the daytime and the three watches of the night all taken up with the struggle against sleep, little time would seem to be left for actual sleep. And when one does nod off, this is to be the occasion for shame. There seems little hope for a good night's rest as long as the passions of the mind afflict us, which is pretty much all the days of our lives. The oversight is too obvious to be unintentional. The image of shame as a robe of honor only seems to reinforce the paradox.

In fact, the point is as simple as it is radical: the quest for clarity of mind should know no limits, but reach down even to the nonconscious, autonomic delusions of the mind at sleep. C. G.

Jung was fond of quoting Augustine to the effect: "I thank God that I am not responsible for my dreams." The allusion is probably apocryphal, but the opinion is common enough. The Buddha rejects the exemption. No less common is the view that the liberated mind is one that has nothing to be ashamed of. This, too, the Buddha rejects as self-flattery. As long as the mind is clouded, there is *everything* to be ashamed of. For one who does not know shame, a good night's sleep only adds to the delusion.

The shift away from the supremacy of the rule that we noted above becomes more evident as the instruction continues:

> My dear monks, even if someone were to come along and cut off your limbs one by one, you should compose your mind and clear it of all spite. Not a harsh word should cross your lips. If you let animosity have its way, it will block the path you have chosen and take the virtue out of your meritorious deeds. *No keeping of the rule or taking up ascetical practices can accomplish what forbearance can.* One who practices it deserves to be called a tower of strength. One who cannot cheerfully accept the poison of scorn and derision like a vial of sweet nectar does not deserve to be called a follower of the Way and a lover of wisdom.

After all the attention given to what the rule *can* do, here we are told that it *cannot* do what the virtue of forbearance can, that taking responsibility for the rule requires insight into the limits of the rule. Set in the context of a widely circulated (though probably erroneous) legend about the immediate cause of the Buddha's death, the teaching takes on added significance. For the same Buddha who is explaining to his monks the meaning and importance of the rule is himself dying of food poisoning contracted by eating a bad piece of liver—an obvious infraction of the rule against eating meat.

Whatever else his instructions may say, they cannot but communicate the message that fixation on regulations only further clouds the mind that the rule is meant to clear. Rather than fear the poison that can kill the body, one ought to fear the poison that can kill the soul. This is the sense in which, without forbearance for the weaknesses of others, the rule intoxicates:

The reason is this: bitterness destroys what is good and true, and effaces one's honor. Nobody in this world or the next likes to see it. You must realize that a heart filled with spite is worse than a fierce fire. Be ever on guard lest it happen to you. *Nothing robs you of virtue like bitterness.* One may be more forgiving of such animus in the white-robes in the world who do not undertake the monastic life. But it is inconceivable that one could walk the way of the monk and be filled with bitterness and spite, any more than a fiery bolt of lightning can issue from a clear blue sky.

At first glance the image of holiness we have so far is one of little passion and great passivity. Subservience to the rule, the reining in of sensuality, and the profound sense of shame are reinforced by the cultivation of long-suffering and an insensitivity to personal affront bordering on autism. By comparison, even the benighted path of the white-robed lay believers seems more spiritually appealing. But slowly the way is being prepared for the recovery of the highest pleasure. The next instruction, a short one, brings us a step closer to the core of the sūtra:

My good monks, take your hand and run it over your head. You have left behind all ornamentation in dress for coarse-colored robes, and taken up your bowls to beg for your needs. As for your self-esteem, I have this to say: when you feel conceit in you, dispose of it quickly. Letting arrogance batten and grow strong in you is far worse for a monk than it is for a white-robe in the world. Those who have left their homes to walk the way of the monk must rather, in the name of the deliverance they seek, learn to humble their minds and beg. And if you find yourself fawning on others, dear monks, know that you are walking on the wrong path. Clear your mind of all pretense and carry on, for flattery can only twist the mind into self-deceit. It is not permitted to the monk. Therefore, I urge you to keep your minds upright and seek that which matters—honestly and without pretense.

The passage may bring a smile to the face of the modern reader; not so for the Buddha's disciples. For the mind that grows proud of its achievements and forgets to look at itself also forgets where it is and where it is "headed." The Buddha simply tells the monks to run their hands where their hair used to be and remember—as if looking into an inner mirror—what is most important.

The injunctions against pretense reach beyond the monastic rule, as we see in the following section.

THE AIM OF VIRTUE

The second part of the sūtra complements the first by providing the wider context against which the monastic vocation of leaving the world makes sense, the context in which the boundaries between world and monastery fall aside and the rule opens up into a universal ethic. In reading the text this way, I assume a stance directly opposed to the traditional explanation which seems to see the first part as more universal in application, and the second as more immediately "religious" and hence aimed at practice by the monks.[12]

In particular, the instruction introduces a series of eight specific virtues to be cultivated, beginning with the limiting of desire:

Dear monks, consider what it means to desire much. *As many as the benefits one seeks are the passions that afflict the mind in the seeking.* The person of few desires seeks nothing, wants nothing, and thus is free of affliction. But even if one's desires are few, discipline is still necessary, for to limit one's desires produces much of virtue and merit. One whose desires are few does not stoop to curry favors of others or yield to the lure of the senses. *The practice of limiting one's desires brings the mind a sense of composure free of all anxiety.* However many things one comes into contact with, they never leave a sense of insufficiency. To have but few desires is to have nirvana. This is what is meant by desiring little.

As we noted above, the injunction against fawning on others and currying favor forms a bridge from the first part of the sūtra to the second. Now the reason becomes clear: the mind that has been brought under control by forsaking license must guard against the return of license in the form of privileges granted by others. The satisfaction the Buddha has in mind to teach his followers is one *without privilege or license.*

The discipline of desire is not perfected in the restraint of desire, but rather produces its best fruits after the restraint has taken effect. The control of desire is not an achievement but a starting point. It is an experiment in a new way of seeing, empowered by desire concentrated on what really matters:

> My dear monks, if it is your desire to escape the passions of the mind, you must give some thought to sufficiency. *The principle of sufficiency offers a comfortable, secluded spot.* One who knows how much is enough is comfortable even if made to sleep on the ground; one who does not is uneasy in the very courts of heaven. For one who can never have enough, wealth is still poverty; for one who knows what it is to have enough, there is wealth even in poverty.[13] One who does not know how much is enough is forever pulled this way and that by the desires of the senses; one who knows finds consolation. This is what is meant by *knowing how much is enough.*

As the sūtra reaches its climax, the words of the Buddha slip out more easily between the heavy iron bars of translation. For the point is withal uncomplicated and unembellished: *one limits desire in order to enjoy sufficiency.*[14]

The *Sūtra of the Eight Great Awakenings,* a short text composed in Chinese around the second century, includes awakening to the knowledge of sufficiency as the third of the awakenings: "the insight that the mind never wearies of having enough."[15] The mind converted to sufficiency is clear, transparent—and enjoyable. Learning to limit desire is not a lackluster, lowland path between the extremes of worldly gluttony and ascetic self-torture, but a high point from which both these extremes look mediocre.

Nor, as the *Old Sūtra of Collected Analogies* says, is insight into sufficiency a matter of mere "rationing,"[16] replacing greed with carefully calculated frugality. Fixing limits to desire clears the mind so that it can think its best thoughts, savor its greatest delights. A surplus of desire, indeed a surplus of *anything,* be it goods or power or ideas or even religious practice, dissipates one's capacity for enjoyment.[17]

What is more, the principle of sufficiency (literally here, "the law of knowing how much is enough") is a kind of spiritual alchemy for turning desire into *con-solation,* for turning anxiety into *com-posure* and pain into *com-fort.* Far from isolating one from the human community, a knowledge of sufficiency is the foundation for true conviviality. In the words of an early Chinese sūtra that deals with many of the same topics:

> Knowing how much is enough—this is conviviality.[18]

The pursuit of the religious path is normally taken to be the solitary path par excellence. The pride of being free—at least since modern times—is something we naturally associate with the ability to "make up one's own mind." But in fact we never make up our own minds. We are always and ever a part of one another's minds, and it is in the community of minds that we find our highest spiritual satisfaction. This should be kept in mind as the text goes on to discuss the meaning of the withdrawal into solitude:

> My dear monks, if what you seek is a serenity free of all the things there are to do, take yourself away from the buzzing confusion to a place where you can be alone. *One who abides in quiet retreat has the admiration of Powerful Lord Indra.*

The appearance of a god from Hindu mythology is somewhat arresting at first. Indra, called the Powerful (Śakra) because of his conquest of the sea demon who tried to control the waters, rides the heavens, thunderbolts in hand, splitting the clouds asunder each spring to bring rain to the parched earth. For a country like India, which has known the devastations of drought throughout the centuries, a god who controls the rain is a natural image for a supreme Doer. The Buddha's image of nirvanic mind is the exact opposite—a deliberate letting go of action, a kind of "doing without doing."

The business of life, whatever the object of one's attention happens to be at a given time, is to keep busy. *This* is what the Buddha's teaching of nirvana aims to refute by speaking of a state in which one can *be* without always having something to *do*. This may seem less than our normal image of what makes a life worth living, but if one thinks of such a state as "clearing" the mind so that one can reconsider all one's doings, then it is an ideal *without which* we would be less than fully human. The conclusion follows naturally:

> *Therefore, let go of family and society, and go empty into solitude if you would root out the cause of suffering.* As many as your pleasures are, so many shall your pains be. If many birds flock to a great tree, they will weigh down heavily on it until it weakens and breaks. The restraints of society welter one into misery until, like an old elephant stuck in the mud, there is no getting out. This is why we speak of *withdrawal.*

As hinted at earlier, the idea of withdrawal into solitude need not be taken only in the literal sense of a monk's hermitage. Like English, Buddhist Chinese uses the image of "dwelling" also for "dwelling on" ideas that have us mired down in the mud of convention. The art of solitude is linked with three virtues, all of which have to do with clearing the mind so that it can see, and none of which, to repeat, are specifically identified with the life of the monk:

> If you make the effort, dear monks, and put your spirit to it diligently, nothing is too difficult. So do it. Even a little water can wear down a rock if it keeps at it long enough. *The discipline of gradually emancipating the mind is like fire-drilling a tree.* No matter how badly you want a fire, it is going to be hard to get a fire going if you stop before it gets hot enough. This is what is meant by a *diligent spirit.*

My dear monks, seek good friends and good helpers. Avoid forgetfulness. Without forgetfulness to delude you, there is no way for
the passions of the mind to get in and rob you. Therefore, always
keep your thoughts collected. If you lose recollection, you forfeit
virtue, but if your mind is firm in its resolve, not even the thieving
passions of the mind will do you harm. If you enter the fray harnessed in armor, you have nothing to fear. This is what is known as
not forgetting.

A recollected mind, dear monks, is a mind that is centered. And a
mind that is centered is able to see through the things of life to the
law of life-and-death. So always be diligent in your practice of cultivating virtue. The concentrated mind does not let itself become
scattered. Like a household that shores up its banks in order to
conserve water, the disciple cultivates meditative concentration to
keep the waters of wisdom from running off wastefully. This is
what is known as *centering.*

The ideal of a clear mind, dwelling in serenity, is anything but
an anesthetized mind, 5,000 feet beyond pleasure and pain. The
virtues of diligence, recollection, and centering are not to be cultivated for their own sake, any more than is the principle of
sufficiency. Like the rejection of privilege and license, they are
meant to ease the disease of our existence, to increase the pleasures of life. Wisdom begins with insight into limits:

My dear monks, *if you have wisdom you will not be consumed by
greed.* Continued self-reflection will keep you from straying. With
it, you will find emancipation in the midst of people and things.
Without it, you have already shut yourself out of the monkhood.
Indeed, you cannot even be numbered among the white-robes.
You can only be called dislocated. Wisdom is the sturdy bark that
will carry you across the sea of old age, sickness, and death. It is a
torch shining brightly in the dark night of ignorance. It is good
medicine for all that ails you, a sharp axe to fell the passions of the
mind. Therefore, good monks, listen, think, and discipline your
mind that wisdom may grow and thrive in you. One who has the

light of wisdom can see things clearly even without the gift of divine sight. This is what is meant by *wisdom*.

There is nothing supernatural about the wisdom to which the Buddha exhorts his followers, nor is it restricted to those of the monk's calling. It is not a wisdom that can be learned simply by reading the sūtras. Indeed, it is not a body of ideas at all but a *habit of thinking clearly* that illumines whatever it turns its attention to. In other words, the principle of sufficiency and the art of satisfaction are not techniques to be mastered and certified by experts. They are wisdom in practice. This is what is meant by virtue.

Now if it is true that wisdom begins by seeing through the dark ignorance of conventional wisdom, it must not allow itself to be waylaid by pointless academic debate either, as the next brief instruction tells us:

> My dear monks, if you let yourselves in for all sorts of frivolous sophistry, your minds will only become scattered. You may have left home, but this does not mean you are liberated. So let go of such academic games as harass the mind. If you desire the pleasure of nirvanic peace, obliterate them all. This is what is meant by the *obliteration of sophistry*.

THE PERFECTION OF VIRTUE

The third section of the sūtra ties the first and second sections together in a simple exhortation to appropriate the truth:

> My dear monks, to give oneself wholeheartedly to the rejection of license through the practice of these virtues is like ridding oneself of a vengeful thief. All desire for the blessings of the World Honored One's[19] great compassion require supreme effort. You have only to exert yourself in practice. Whether you are in the mountains or the marshlands, under a tree, in a solitary retreat or in a quiet room, think of the Dharma you have received and never lose sight of it.

Always exert yourselves, be diligent in spirit, and practice the Dharma. If you do not, your death will be in vain, and you will rue it later. *Like a good doctor, I have made my diagnosis and explained the cure, but it is not up to me whether you take your medicine or not.* The good guide can only guide well, but it is not the fault of the guide if people do not listen and walk the Way for themselves.

The three concluding sections of the sūtra, comprising roughly one-fifth of the whole, depict the Buddha taking leave of life. After repeating the simple message of his very first sermon—the famous diagnosis and remedy for the disease of human existence known as the Four Noble Truths—he tries to calm the grief of his disciples by showing them that he faces death as a friend, not as a frightful enemy. The effect is to open the text out into the wider Buddhist tradition and at the same time to break the enchantment of the sacred, returning the reader to the everyday world where virtue is to be exercised.[20]

The departure of the teacher, Buddha, is symbolic of the leave-taking that must accompany all discipleship. To throw oneself meditatively, submissively into a text of these proportions is to journey into the unclarity of mind, armed only with an awe of the dark and a desire for seeing more clearly. The Buddha's instructions do little to enhance the satisfaction of having one's house in order. They are rather about the ekstasis of letting go of the conventional order of things. Only then can the quest for the satisfaction of knowing how much is enough, of healing the symbolon, of squaring the circle, become an experiment in refreshing one's imagination of what it means to enjoy a clear mind and life together.

The earliest indication among the ancient Greeks of a universal morality free of tribal and cultural bias is said to be found in two sayings engraved on the walls of Apollo's temple at Delphi: know yourself (γνῶθι σαυτόν) and nothing too much (μὴ δὲν ἄγαν). The great variety of traditions in philosophy, religion, science, and the arts that have taken up the first injunction remain alive and well in modern culture. By comparison the collective human response to the second lags far behind—for the most part uninspired, inarticulate, isolated from the morality of everyday. I suggest we listen to it as a vocation to a higher culture.

NOTES

[1] Subsequently published as "Towards a Principle of Sufficiency," *Zen Buddhism Today* 8 (1990): 152-64.

[2] The translation is repeated, for example, in Harold Stewart, *The Old Walls of Kyoto* (Tokyo: Weatherhill, 1981), 172, where the author even paraphrases it to read "be content with what you have." Similarly, the current Urasenke Grand Tea Master reads the saying as "I only know contentment," citing the phrase 足知安分 (contentment with one's lot) as a Buddhist teaching that is central to the Way of Tea. It seems to me that his interpretation of the phrase to mean the inner peace that comes from "knowing what is enough" is closer to the Buddhist meaning than either the translation or the literary allusion. See Sen Sōshitsu xv, "Knowing Contentment," *Chanoyu Quarterly* 67 (1991):5–6.

In this regard, it should be noted that the donor of the *tsukubai*, Tokugawa Mitsukuni, was a rabid enemy of organized Buddhism and a key figure in the Mito School, which attempted to restore Japanese culture by eliminating all foreign influence. He ordered the destruction of 1,000 Buddhist temples in order to have Shinto shrines built in their place, sparing only those of historical value. Although said to have been a pious Buddhist in his private life, he rejected the custom of shaving his head and assuming a Buddhist name upon retirement from public office. His donation of the *tsukubai* to the temple suggests that he did not himself consider the saying to be distinctively Buddhist.

[3] I have found Charles Taylor's splendid book, *Sources of the Self* (Cambridge: Harvard University Press, 1989), of great value in connecting the problem of the modern self with traditional ethical concerns. A few years after the publication of the present essay, I did in fact take up the question of the reified Self in "The Quest of the True Self: Jung's Rediscovery of a Modern Invention." *Journal of Religion* 77/2 (1997): 252–67.

[4] William James, *Varieties of Religious Experience* (New York: Modern Library, 1902), 498.

[5] T.12.389, 1110a–1112b. Apparently an English translation was done by Nukariya Kaiten and privately published in Tokyo in 1897, but even with the kind assistance of the keepers of his library, it has proved impossible to track down.

[6] A partial translation of the work appears in Edward Conze's *Buddhist Scrip-*

tures (Hardmondsworth: Penguin, 1959), 34-66. For a full text, see vol. 49 of *Sacred Books of the East*, ed. by Max Müller (Delhi: Motilal Banarsidass, 1978).

[7] A reliable translation of the work can be had in John Ross Carter and Mahinda Palihawadana, *The Dhammapada: A New English Translation with the Pali Text* (New York: Oxford University Press, 1987).

[8] *Lao-tzu Te-Tao Ching*, trans. with commentary by Robert G. Henricks (New York: Ballantine, 1989), 85, 13.

[9] The text cited here appears also in the 出曜経 *Sūtra of Departure from the Everyday* (T. 4.732a), a Chinese rendition of the *Udānavarga*, a lengthy Sanskrit translation and commentary on the *Dhammapada*. My translation draws on the commentary in the surrounding text for the wording.

[10] *The Dhammapada*, 257.

[11] *The Udānavarga, Sūtra of Departure from the Everyday*. Section 23 bears the title "Stepping out of the Mud" of social convention.

[12] See the *Kokuyaku issaikyō* 国一切経, vol. 3 of the "Collected Sūtras," 146, note 45.

[13] In the *Treatise of Grand Sublimity*, attributed to Aśvaghoṣa and translated by the same Kumārajīva, the same point is made the other way around: "To one who does not know how much is enough, wealth is poverty" (T.4.267c).

[14] This is the sense of the four Chinese characters 少欲足知. Though not found as a unit in the text discussed here, the phrase is a common one in early sūtras and commentaries. The Chinese translation of a passage in the *Buddhacarita* (12.47) uses it this way: "Make your desires few and stop when you are satisfied.... Enjoy the discipline of solitude in a place apart" (T.4.23b).

[15] T.17.715b.

[16] T.4.517c.

[17] The Tendai scholar Paul Swanson has drawn my attention to a passage in the *Shorter T'ien-tai Manual of Contemplation* (T.46.463a) which states this specifically. An early Chinese sūtra that draws on the *Dhammapada* tradition, *Sūtra of the Essentials of the Dharma*, also makes a direct link between knowing sufficiency as giving nirvanic satisfaction and making it possible to enter into meditation. (See also T.4.783c).

[18] *Sūtra of the Former Lives of the Buddha*, T.4.108a. The Chinese has 足知人間楽, suggesting that it is not merely the individual who knows how much is enough (足知之人) but the community of such persons whose lives are made enjoyable by application of the principle of sufficiency. The sanctification of the community of monks as one of the three jewels of Buddhism, the "bodhisattva

ideal" as the selfless compassion of the awakened mind for others, and the image of the community of "countless Buddhas" that figures prominently in the *Lotus Sūtra* all militate against the idea that the enlightened mind is a mind isolated in self-enjoyment.

[19] The Buddha is referring to himself here.

[20] The final statement recalls a passage in the *Buddhacarita,* the legendary life of the Buddha referred to earlier. "It is not enough to look at the doctor; one must take the medicine to be cured." See Conze, 62 (translation adjusted).

Make-Believe Nature

In December, 1992, a group of citizens in the city of Seto in central Japan organized a meeting at the town hall to protest plans by the prefectural government to "develop" a natural preserve as a proposed site for an International Expo in the year 2005. The Seto Nature Association, one of the principal organizers of the meeting, had despaired of a fair hearing in the business community, which stood to gain most from the event, and decided to rally support to halt the plans. I was invited to address the question of what has happened to "nature" in the contemporary imagination and welcomed the opportunity to toss another sabot into the works.

Several of the most active participants in the protest—which is still going on—were long-time members of a series of public seminars I had been conducting for some ten years on the estrangement of religion from immediate experience, work, technology, and the primacy of the natural world.

Rather than simply focus on the concrete question at hand, I tried to look at the way in which the very idea of nature itself has been reified and then surrounded with an aura of sentimentality in contemporary Japanese society. It seemed to me that it would not be enough to postpone the destruction of the natural preserve or to relocate the Expo to another site.

I wanted to suggest in direct but simple terms that those taking opposite sides in a particular conflict can nonetheless share a common myth towards nature.

The talk was published under the title「自然と心」『出会い』 [Encounter] 11/3 (1994): 44–54. The English translation reproduced here appeared in the *Japan Christian Review* 59 (1993): 103–11.

GIVEN THE CURRENT progress of civilization's onslaught against the natural world, only a refusal to look at the facts can allow a people to compliment itself any longer on its love of nature. Such self-flattery is based on a distinctively modern habit of thought that I will call the "sentimentalization of nature." In conclusion I will offer a few concrete proposals for breaking the habit. Before doing so, I know of no better way to shed light on what has in effect become a mass addiction to a make-believe nature than to talk circles around the problem—like a hawk playing with a sparrow, driving it higher and higher until it runs out of breath and can be taken hold of effortlessly. It is not that the point of what I have to say is too complex, but that it is almost too simple and its gravity too evasive to grasp at first swipe.

I

The *sentimentalization of nature* is a phenomenon that takes different forms in different cultures. But it also cuts across traditional cultural borderlines and indeed has become one of the mainstays of the process of "internationalization" that has resulted in what we are now accustomed to call "global culture."

The dominant cultural attitude toward nature today conforms to a uniform measure of the quality of life that we may call "economic-developmental." Our ideal of the good life, and the way it has led us to look at the natural world, is all but blind to distinctions of agricultural and industrial, rich and poor, warring and peaceful, democratic and despotic. It flows along in the modern mind beneath the surface of our weightier daily preoccupations. Indeed, it is only by tacit agreement to leave this attitude just beneath the surface of awareness that we can embrace it without having to think about whether it is morally acceptable or not.

Simply put, the dominant cultural attitude toward nature has two defining traits. First, it values nature primarily as a nourishing, livable, enjoyable environment for human beings; and devalues nature when it proves to be a hostile, disobedient, malnourishing environment for human beings. In order to promote the former and gradually eliminate the latter, civilized communities have assumed the *right* to adjust and transform the world that surrounds them. This right is mitigated only by the accompanying moral *duty* to assure that human persons, and not mere economic profit, are given first place of honor. Should circumstances face a people with a choice, however, between the health and preservation of animal and plant species on the one hand and human wellbeing on the other, this same morality obliges them to sacrifice the nonhuman world for the sake of the human.

Second, the dominant attitude toward nature holds that human understanding of the natural world progresses by trial and error, building on its past achievements and mending its past misbehavior as it goes. When some unforeseen or unfortunate damage is done to the natural world by the application of new technologies to human work, damage that might actually affect humans adversely, the assumption is that further investment of time and scientific research will teach our trained experts how to right the wrong and insure us against its repetition. Moreover, if the generation of new tools and methods to correct the abuses and oversights of the old is made economically profitable, there is every reason to believe that technology will remain at the service of people and not the other way around. However, in adverse economic situations, where too much attention to the devastations technology has inflicted on the natural world might threaten overall economic development, concern with the environment has occasionally to be compromised or postponed.

These two ideas—that nature is our lawful environment and that technological excesses can be repaired by further technology—are at the root of the human-centered philosophy underlying development. I referred to this earlier as a *common sense,* but when we turn to the world of fact, of what has actually happened in the name of this philosophy of ours, we see it to be a dangerous *common nonsense* of ecocidal proportions. For all its scientific moorings, our dominant cultural attitude toward nature functions like a myth that cannot be brought into question without harassing the style of life to which we have become accustomed. Instead, public *facta* about the state of the natural world are transfigured into political *agenda* to be taken up or postponed at the convenience of our elected leadership, while common sense is left to bear the affront by making do with a make-believe world. The willing participation in this conspiracy is facilitated by what I am calling the sentimentalization of nature.

Consider, for example, the fact that the words "clean air" no longer correspond to anything concrete in nature. There is simply no more clean air anywhere on earth—not in the depths of the great rain forests, not on the ice-caps of the north pole—that does not bear the smudge of industrial waste. This has been common scientific knowledge for a decade and more.

But now a group of young people take advantage of a long week-end to get away from the soot and cement of the city into the clean, green world of nature. They walk for hours into the mountains and pitch camp in a small woods. Awakening in the early morning to the chirping of the birds and the rustle of the trees, one of them climbs to the summit of a nearby hill. As the sun rises in the east he fills his lungs with the fresh, clean air and feels himself cleansed body and soul from the sickness of everyday life. Were he to pause and consult his knowledge, he would realize that the air he is taking in carries the same damaging elements as the air in the city, only in lesser quantities; and that the work whose wages paid for this escape into nature is contributing generously to the impurification. But nothing is quite so devastating to the rapture of natural beauty as the heartless invasion of facts, and so he wraps his conscience in the innocence of make-believe, and allows the moment instead to reconfirm his faith in civilization: nature is *our* environment, and as long as we remember that, one day a way will be found to make the air clean for us to breathe again.

Aristotle opens his *Metaphysics* with the words, "All people, by nature, desire to know." The accumulation of knowledge and the relentless drive of the scientific spirit seem to demonstrate how right he was. The way we sentimentalize nature, however, tells us the opposite: all of us also desire by nature *not to know*. What we do not want to know is that there is simply no longer any place for us to go to "get away from it all." Wherever we are, the poison of civilization is right there with us.

The consequences of dirty air turn out to be far more radical than anyone could have imagined. During our own lifetimes, the weather has permanently changed, so much so that previous meteorological records have become all but irrelevant for forecasting. There is no turning back from this state of affairs. There is nothing that can be done to undo the damage. No future technology can alter this fact any more than it can bring back the thousands of species of plants and animals lost to "progress." When a tree that has stood longer than human civilization itself is felled to build a highway so that people can commute faster to work, the mourning is left to a powerless few. For the rest, it is enough to remember that, after all, it is *our* world and someday, given the chance, we will fix it.

Whatever cultural or spiritual values the weekend gardener might have in mind when building a little garden or raising a few flowers and vegetables, it can no longer be a question of "doing one's part" for the cultivation of the natural world. The civilized management of nature has long since broken away from metaphors of tending one's garden. The backyard flower-patch no longer mirrors a larger cultural reality, and therefore no longer nourishes a state of soul that has anything to do with the way we manage nature. It is sentimental make-believe.

When I said that the facta of nature became political agenda, I did not mean to imply that our governments do not reflect the will of the people. There is no national government anywhere in the world prepared to offer its voting citizens the choice of putting their nation's economic progress, their personal and corporate wealth, second to the protection of nature. A vote for nature would be tantamount to a vote against civilization, which no modern society is willing to tolerate. At the same time, there is no government that does not require its children to study in school the facts of environmental problems that make this very choice more and more inevitable. Sentimentalism is no longer a private matter, like taking a vacation from the factory to breathe pure mountain air or raising a garden to demonstrate one's love of nature. It is a chosen way of life for which there appear to be no alternatives.

Because this dominant attitude toward nature is a global convention, the cultural differential shows up only in the *forms of expression that our sentimentalism takes.* Cultural attitudes towards nature are no longer distinguished primarily by present patterns of thought and behavior as by diversity of historical pasts which sets one culture off from another. What is particularly Japanese about the Japanese people's attitude toward nature, for instance, today belongs to a way of life that has ceased to exist, to a way of thinking and behaving that once was but no longer is. Insofar as one's sense of cultural distinctiveness fails to distinguish fact from make-believe, it indulges itself in a kind of sentimentalism that savors the wonders and terrors of nature without so much as a thought to the contradictions this raises for daily life.

The sentimental habits that make the eyes water just enough to blear the vision of nature represent a kind of global addiction masquerading as local custom. When one drives to a well-lit and heated cultural center to practice *haiku* or *ikebana* in the belief that one is doing something of age-old cultural significance, one is also consenting to believe what one has been made to believe, ignoring the facts one knows to be true. What was once a spiritual exercise now requires for its practice a state of mind that turns the eye to a nature that does not exist by turning the eye away from the nature that does—a nature that is there to see at the exhaust coming out of the tail pipe or the wastebaskets full of half-used paper. It matters not whether one defines one's country as developed or developing. Sentimentalization renders impotent once dominant cultural attitudes towards trees, animals, air, water, and soil, and in their place leaves a shimmering but empty fantasy.

What needs to be done is clear to any schoolchild faced with the acts of civilized life at the dawn of the twenty-first century. First, and most important, we need to "let nature be nature," to stop wounding what has lived for aeons before human progress began infecting the planet. Then—and *only* then—have we to begin repairing the cultures that contributed to this wounding.

II

Culture, as the word has classically been understood, is the balance that a community of people strikes between *cultivatio* and *cultus*, between efforts to make nature over and reverence for the divinity of what nature does on its own. This is not to say that the work of remaking nature to sustain and enhance human life was ever experienced, even in the most primitive of societies, as a harmonious cooperation between a people and their Gods. Displeasure at the unreliability of nature, even when ascribed to the interference of heavenly powers, seems to have been behind the aspiration to tool-making throughout human history. Thus as tools became more and more efficient for managing the environment, reliance on the rule of the Gods over the natural world weakened correspondingly. Often enough this led to reinforcing belief in the sway of divine destiny over the trials and blessings of human life, so that the gradual transformation of nature into a human environment was mirrored in a comparable transformation of the Gods into a Divine Providence ruling over human history but driven out of nature's story.

This is not the place to go into detail. The only point I wish to make is that the transition from agriculture and animal husbandry to industrial manufacturing, from cultivation to fabrication, was hardly an unexpected shock to the soul. Its requisite spirituality had been brewing almost from the start of civilization and harbored problems far more momentous than simply that of who should control the means of production and what was an equitable relation of work to profit.

At the time of the industrial revolution, a new belief in the efficacy of the division of labor, and its accompanying disassociation of the individual worker from the final product, was promoting the environmentalization of nature both too quickly and too subtly to be noticed. While theologians and philosophers were debating over redrawing the boundaries between science and religion, manufacturing technology was busy forging a new culture of life and work indoors. Progress in the control of temperature and lighting created not only a new climate for the uninterrupted manufacture of goods, but lent support to a universal creed of progress that viewed the natural world as an inexhaustible resource for enhancing the lifestyle of the human community.

It is in the context of this history that I believe we have to view our current habits of sentimentalizing nature. It bears recalling, too, that the world of nature has not suffered the transformations of this history gallantly. However "natural" it seems to us to imagine the nonhuman world as a collection of laws and reproductive codes, the sickness that the world has contacted in the name of human progress—in some measure, already a sickness unto death—has turned the dream of an environmentalized nature into a human nightmare. The technological reliefs available to the wealthier countries, who consider themselves more "developed" because of the quality of their life indoors, are by and large closed off to the "undeveloped," who must suffer the increasing revenge of life outdoors. What makes our modern sentimentalization of nature morally unacceptable is precisely that the nature we enjoy in packaged doses, whose wonders and mysteries we applaud in art and poetry and religion, is a luxury item paid for by continued abuse of nature. Nor should the irony be lost on us that these same abuses pay for our gathering here in this hall today to lament what is happening.

Against this background, the injunction to "let nature be nature" is nothing other than a call to put a halt to the environmentalization of nature. Nature has no choice but to be what it is. As the Sino-Japanese term *shizen* 自然 suggests, it is the nature of nature to work of itself, without relying on anything outside of itself. Now that we have seen how nature exercises that choice against the aggressions of human technology, we must renounce the dream of taking that choice away from nature. It is not a question of something we can do or might do if only we can muster the will—it is something we *must* do.

For my part, I see this obligation beginning with the resuscitation in modern consciousness of a number of very old and very simple ideas, pulling them up from our past slowly enough so that we can see just where we lost touch with them. One of those ideas, and one dear to the heart of much oriental art and culture, is the idea of "the usefulness of being useless." There is a story in the "Inner Chapters" of the *Chuang-tsu* that speaks to the point eloquently and offers a good starting point for tracing the story of our distraction from respect for the natural world. It is a story about a certain master carpenter named Stone and his apprentice, and how they happened one day to encounter the truth about useless trees.

It seems that on one of their voyages the two chanced to pass by a gigantic oak tree standing by a local village shrine. The young apprentice stopped short and stood aghast at the towering majesty of the tree, whose trunk he thought must measure a hundred spans in girth, and whose branches were so immense that at least ten of them could be carved into boats. But the carpenter Stone just stalked off ahead without so much as giving the tree a second glance. Catching his master up, the apprentice inquired why he should have shunned such a chance for timber, more splendid than any he had seen since taking up his axe.

"Stop it!" the master rebuked him. "The tree is useless. A boat made from it would sink, a coffin would soon rot, a tool would split, a door would ooze sap, and a beam would have termites. It is worthless timber and is of no use to us. That is why it has reached such a ripe old age."

That night the oak tree appeared to carpenter Stone in a dream and complained of being compared with useful trees that are stripped and pruned and robbed of their fruits or cut down in their prime because they attract the attentions of the common world.

"As for me," said the great tree, "I have been trying for a long time to be useless. I was almost destroyed several times, but at last I have found a way to become useless, and this the most useful thing of all. If I had been useful, could I have ever grown so large? Besides, you and I are both things. How can one thing judge another thing? What does a dying and worthless man like you know about a worthless tree?"

The next day, when the apprentice heard of the dream, he was puzzled. "If the tree had so great a desire to be useless, why does it serve as a shrine?" This time the master took up the cause of the tree. "It is just pretending to be a sacred tree so that it will not be hurt by those who do not know that it is useless. If it had not, it would probably have been cut down. It protects itself in a different way from ordinary things. We will miss the point if we judge it in the ordinary way."

The story reaches across the ages from ancient China in the third century BCE to our own with so little loss of power that it is almost superfluous to comment on it. The oak tree speaks to us directly of a nature that struggled then, as it does now, to be useless to human civilization. It enjoins us, as it did carpenter Stone, to find it in our hearts to let nature be nature.

But there is one detail in the story, easy to pass over on a first reading, to which I would like to draw your attention: the tree found its uselessness in serving as a sacred tree. For carpenter Stone, this was no more than its way of protecting itself from misunderstanding by pretending to be something that people could understand. But surely there is more. The "shrine" in which it stood was a traditional sacred grove set apart in nature by a local community for worship, a place where they could invoke the blessings of the Gods and beg their protection against the ravages of nature. As such, it represented limits to the usefulness of nature in creating a human environment. The Gods were believed to watch over the human world because they were privy to the higher purposes of an apparently useless nature.

Belief in the uselessness of nature as mediating the relationship between the human and divine is a fundamental religious fact that has taken a great variety of forms throughout history. In the biblical myth of creation, God created nature out of nothing. Nature was not made out of God nor even out of the same stuff as God, but was generated by a word ordering it into existence. From the beginning there was no natural bond between what was created and the one who created it. The moral law that set human beings apart from the rest of nature and gave them a sense of sin was also established by divine decree. Immorality was an offense against a higher reality that transcended the natural world, whose commandments began with an uncompromising stricture against revering as divine what were no more than idols of the natural world.

That the philosophical criticism of Western civilization which followed on the heels of the Industrial Revolution should have included a pronouncement of the death of the transcendent God of creation in modern consciousness is hardly to be wondered at. Nor is it surprising that in our own day, where the echoes of that pronouncement ring louder than ever, a renewed interest in polytheism should have flooded in to fill the spiritual gap. The irony is that the "new polytheism," as it is called, is still largely viewed as an archetypal reality of the psyche or as some kind of phenomenon of the spirit world. The cultural critique aimed at the cult of a transcendent divinity does not yet seem to have reached a critique of the excesses wrought by the cultivation of the natural.

Seen in the context of a general history of religions, Japan's myth of creation is rather more typical—and in that sense closer also to the kind of myth the Genesis account was pitted against. There Gods and humans are believed to have come from the same stuff, as we read in the first lines of the *Nihongi*, born of a common chaotic mass. To walk the earth is to be in touch not only with our ancestors but with the Gods. Despite Japan's equally sophisticated and culturally important myths of creation, evolutionary theory did not cause the religious upheaval here that it did in the Christian West. For one thing, the distinction between literal truth and symbolic truth never developed in classical Oriental cultures, so that demythologization never posed much of a threat to religious belief. But equally important, the special relationship between the divine and the human never seemed to require transcendence of the natural world.

This does not mean that there is no equivalent to the "death of God" in modern Japanese consciousness. There is, and from the standpoint of the natural world, it is of greater historical moment than its counterpart in the West. For the *Kami* of Japan have become no more than ornaments of modern nostalgia, their powers harnessed to the economic forces that move modern life and determine what is of value in it. If one does not hear talk of the death of the Kami in Japan, it is because they are dying not through assault but through neglect, a form of murder too civilized to be even aware of its own deed.

To read what Japan has to say of its own spirituality, one would think—and there are many who do in fact think just this— that here is a fully modern society to which the claim of the ancient Greek philosopher Thales continues to apply: "all things are full of Gods." In actuality, the Gods of ancient Japan continue to fall victim, one by one, to the same sentimentality that glosses the surface of Japan's ongoing contributions to the devastation of the natural world.

I have a finely crafted table made of nara wood in my home. To touch it is to know that it houses a Kami. But the formica desk at which I work each day is completely godless. No one would give a second thought to the idea that there might be a Kami in the styrofoam cups that fall out of the vending machine on the corner, but neither would anyone fail to recognize the Kami in the *chawan* that sits on my shelf. Removing the irregularities of nature and the fingerprints of the human artisan from the artifacts may have contributed to quality control of mass-produced goods, but it also severed a bond between us and the Gods that leaves us much the worse for it all.

The size of the population which modern civilization has to service seems to make these losses seem minor or at least unavoidable, but it is more than a matter of adjusting to formica desks and styrofoam cups. We have come to accept the permanent disfiguration of nature brought about by rampant gluttony for manufactured goods as a matter of course. The pattern is ever and again the same. A small wood is leveled to the ground and cement is poured for a new road to alleviate traffic congestion, or rather to transfer the focal point of the congestion to some other as yet untouched patch of nature. The deed is then crowned ceremoniously by planting a new row of trees along the sides of the road as a tribute to the "natural environment." But the trees are no replacement at all. They are no more than denatured, godless parts of the traffic system, each standing like a tombstone to a Kami that has given up its spirit so that civilization might live better.

The systematic banishment of the Kami from nature has left its own spiritual vacuum, which (perhaps because the deed has gone so completely unnoticed) has tended to fill up with ideas of the divine imported from elsewhere in the developed world. The sentimentalization of an abused nature is not unconnected with current fashions in Japanese religiosity in which the spirit world, the psychology of the unconscious, the search for information about one's former lives, out-of-the-body and out-of-life experiences, and the like have moved from periphery to center.

Whatever personal benefits may accrue to the individual as a result of all this, on a broader cultural plane it is but another sanction to the banishment of the Kami from nature, demonstrating yet again the poverty and utter naivete of the Meiji-era ideal of "Japanese soul, Western know-how." This is why I see no other path of salvation from the conspiracy of sentimentalization against nature than one that resolutely refuses to view the past through the lenses of today's common sense and seeks rather to look at the present anew, as if for the first time, through the eyes of the past.

III

However high the hawk might fly to drive its prey out of breath and take it in its grasp, it cannot fly above itself. In the end, it must return to the earth to nest, and so must we. I conclude my considerations today, therefore, with three simple and serious, if also somewhat ironic, proposals.

First, I propose that the Japanese Federation of Economic Organizations (*Keidanren*) establish a prize comparable in amount to the Nobel Peace Prize in recognition of outstanding contributions to the cause of ecology. The prize might fittingly be named after Bashō, the world-honored *haiku* poet who understood that the primary environment was nature's, not ours. The reason for proposing the Keidanren as the sponsor of the prize is that this group seems best to represent the actual economic powers that at present produce 24% of the world's heavy machinery and 26% of its automobiles. Since the ruling myths of self-identity in Japan seem to share a common belief that its indigenous morality is based on "shame" rather than on the "sin-and-guilt" of Western cultures, it is hard to think of any method better suited to halting the arm that brandishes such a formidable array of weapons against the world of nature than to bring the warriors to shame themselves into an act of virtue.

Second, in line with plans to decentralize the government of Tokyo, and as part of the celebrations accompanying the transfer of the Northern Territories from Russia to Japan, I propose that the Ministry of Education be transferred to the islands immediately upon their return. The move would contribute considerably to the liberation of the Ministry from its captivity to modes of thought which victimize the very world of nature that has figured so importantly in the education of the nation's youth. To live in a city where the instrinsic value of a bush or a tree is overshadowed by the market value of the land on which it stands, where one can be so bound to life indoors that one can go for months, even years, without seeing a sunrise or a sunset, hardly amounts to a healthy environment from which to dictate how young children are to be instructed on the foundations of civilization, the mysteries of the universe and the dignity of life, on literature and musics and the arts. The survival of the natural world depends too radically on the generation now in school to risk anything less in the way of bureaucratic reform.

Third, as residents of one of the richest economies of the world, let those who can actively seek a higher culture based on the rediscovery of a simple life and a deliberate renunciation of current patterns of consumption. The renunciation of luxury I have in mind here is the exact opposite of asceticism as the term is usually understood. I hope to return to this question at a later date, but I have come to think that the range of actual asceticisms inflicted on those who live in developed countries—even if the infliction appears to those in poorer countries to be synonymous with the development they are aiming at—is too high a price to pay for progress. We all know what it is to be trapped by some product or service that modern society advertises as necessary but which actually ends up defrauding one of time, free choice, or even health of mind and body. If one can bring this experience to bear on the expenses and wastes of everyday life, the human environment is certain to look very different: more transparent, less demanding, but perhaps also a greater enemy to the world of nature than one had imagined.

When all is said and done, the necessary change of heart, the resolve to resist the gigantic pressures towards unlimited development of the environment, calls for the very thing that nature itself—the animals and plants, the earth and water and air—have joined in chorus to shout out at us: *Let nature be nature!* We have but to learn to listen.

Catholicizing Health

In the summer of 1997 the first of a series of conferences was held at the initiative of Dr. H. Tristram Engelhardt of the Baylor College of Medicine to discuss the framing of Catholic guidelines to govern intensive hospital care. Given the fact that intensive care accounts for nearly 20 percent of total hopsital service costs in the United States and that good standards exist for assessing the likelihood of patient survival as a result of intensive care, the project seemed to have a solid basis of facts from which to discuss the moral questions involved in providing that care equitably to rich and poor alike.

Despite the special burden that intensive care puts on health budgets in "developing countries," it was felt that the basic moral issues remained the same and that some consensus, therefore, could be reached on common principles.

The following essay is an attempt to question what seemed to me some of underlying assumptions about health, health care, and the nature of moral principles. As a result of the first round of discussions, I have been encouraged to look more closely at some of the ideas expressed very loosely in the pages that follow. I reproduce it here only as a stimulus to have a second look at the certitudes in terms of which we are accustomed to deciding what is a morally acceptable idea of health and what is not.

Originally published, along with the other papers of the project, in T. Engelhardt and M. Cherry, eds., *Allocating Scarce Medical Resources: Roman Catholic Perspectives* (Washington, D. C.: Georgetown University Press, 2002), 297-309.

I WISH TO ARGUE here for an adjustment of the Catholic perspective on technologically intensive medical care. The immediate context for these remarks is the effort under way to produce a set of moral guidelines, based on Catholic principles, to govern the apportionment of limited critical-care facilities to a surplus of patients. I would like to take a step back from the complexities of that question to consider what it means for Catholicism to put the weight of its tradition and institutional presence behind such guidelines. In particular, I mean to suggest that the primary audience for Catholic moral guidance in matters of health has been eclipsed by excessive attention to the problems generated by the medical profession. I have no illusions about the irrelevance of these remarks to the question as framed. No doubt, for many of those who devote themselves to the management of intensive-care units the skepsis in these pages will ring hollow and out of touch with the realities of health care. I ask only that they listen between the lines for the faint echoes of a rising chorus of voices looking for another kind of guidance altogether, and consider whether this clamor is really as secondary a concern for Catholic moral reflection as their professional interests lead them to believe.

QUESTIONING THE MEDICAL MYTHOS

The intensive care unit (ICU) is more than an ensemble of equipment and technicians designed to perform a specific range of tasks for a specific class of patients. It is a metaphor for a wider set of beliefs about the place of science and technology in health. Independently of whom the wires and tubes happen to be attached to at any given moment, the whole kit is permanently attached to a wider network of ideas. Whatever the rate of efficiency of the tools and techniques of the unit, the very fact that it is functioning at all implies a commitment of resources from outside the ICU itself which could have been committed otherwise. And those decisions in turn rest on a set of assumptions and decisions about what things are more valuable than what other things.

For those committed to providing high-tech intensive care, the ICU is an index of the state of medical science as a whole. Whatever goes on within its walls testifies to the level of progress that has been achieved and justifies further expenditure for what has not yet been achieved. This symbolism is real enough, and its meaning is hardly lost on anyone devoted to the betterment of intensive care. But this symbolic meaning is itself wrapped in a wider creed, less clearly articulated, perhaps, but no less firmly adhered to. It is this creed that defines the boundaries for moral concern. In a word, the ICU is assembled, used, and maintained, on the basis of the belief *extra ecclesiam nulla salus*: "no health outside of the system." Though not a blind belief, neither is it without its blind spots.

To anyone with firsthand experience, whether on the giving or receiving end of critical care, it is clear that detachment from the experts and gear assembled in the ICU means all but certain death for the terminally ill whom such units are designed to save. This is why the fact of having more patients than units becomes a moral issue. Whom do we save and whom do we let go? And on what grounds? As long as these units remain at the cutting edge of the healing sciences, there will always be a disproportion of equipment to patients. But the more the question of morality focuses on the appropriate or inappropriate use of available facilities, the stronger grows the conviction that in the best of all possible worlds everyone would have equal access to such treatment. The contradiction is easier to accept than the possibility that the ICU could be grounded on a creed unworthy of belief. In order, therefore, for patients and caretakers to believe that the only real health is health that has been certified by the established medical profession, they must first accept the idea that the presence of scientific validation adds to the value of things, even as its absence devalues things. The ICU is a metaphor of this wider myth.

"Let no one be deceived," writes Origen in the middle of the third century. "Outside this house no one is saved." In matters theological, the words have become by *consensus fidelium* an embarrassment to Catholic tradition, but in matters related to institutionalized medicine they have all but the strength of an infallible dogma. Healing outside of the system is real only by analogy; the history of medicine and diversity of traditional medical practices are valued as a kind of preevangelium. The problem with this creed, as with its soteriological parallels, is not that it aims to be as comprehensive as possible. Neither science nor religion would be served by reining in the will to teach its truth to all nations. The problem is rather that it does not know how to view its own faith except as certitude and how to view other faiths except as heresy. Neither science nor religion is served by this sort of dogmatism.

If the ICU is indeed a metaphor whose significance depends on a broader set of beliefs in the background, a different background implies a shift of meaning in the foreground as well. As ludicrous as it may seem to those who see intensive-care medicine as the best that civilization has to offer humans facing certain death, the fact is, only a minority of the world subscribes to the creed on which it is based. This is not just a reflection of the demographics of technology which relieve most of the world's population of any choice in the matter. There is growing evidence that even those within arm's reach of the latest equipment and methods of medical practice are going through a crisis of faith. In 1997 for the first time the expenditures for alternative therapies in the United States exceeded those paid for primary care services, and the number of actual visits to providers of alternative medicine surpassed that of visits to regular physicians. According to research published in the pages of *The Journal of the American Medical Association*, "Extrapolations to the US population suggest a 47.3% increase in total visits to alternative medicine practitioners, from

427 million in 1990 to 629 million in 1997."[1] The therapies showing the most marked increase include herbal medicine, massage,
megavitamins, self-help groups, folk remedies, energy healing,
and homeopathy. More and more insurance companies are agree-
ing to cover these expenses, and knowledge of alternative medicines is growing among the younger generation of doctors,[2] which
can only further weaken the monopoly of allopathic medicine.
Clearly the myth of scientific medicine that forms the backdrop to
intensive-care medicine may not have quite the hold over the
popular imagination that the medical establishment has taken for
granted.

Trust in the healing powers of one's physicians has long been
known to be a key ingredient in curing illness. Although trust in
prayer and religious faith (which may still be, as Rustom Roy suggests, "the single most powerful pill in the world's pharma-
copoeia"[3]) tend to recede in the modern clinic, it is quickly
replaced by trust in scientific expertise. Still, despite the sophisticated methods at the disposal of doctors today and the vast
amounts of data amassed to put those methods on a solid basis of
objective and verifiable fact, faith in the healing powers of today's
medical profession is far from absolute. And there is no reason to
suspect that better equipment, better medications, better surgical
techniques, and more and more research will ever make it so. As is
the case with all practical science, there will always be cracks in the
method through which superstition and nonscientific ideas can
leak into an otherwise solid trust in the medical profession; as
with all human institutions, there will always be political and economic motives for distracting its functionaries from the highest
aims and full potential of their profession. But rarely does such
mistrust of the establishment touch the core belief in the primacy
of medical science as the guardian of health in an advanced and
civilized society. Nor does the concern with norms for the proper
use of equipment and the proper allocation of resources. More
often they are absorbed into the concern with preserving the

integrity of the profession and weeding out anything that might compromise the fundamental trust of the patient in the system.

The turn to alternative medicine in technologically advanced countries and the continued reliance on traditional medicine in the technologically backward cultures must not be understood simply as the mistaken response of the disillusioned or ignorant. More than a mere loss of faith, it testifies, at least in part, to faith of a different sort altogether. This faith thinks in terms of wholes greater than the sum of body parts; it is not ashamed to talk of forces unknown to and uncontrollable by reason; it values felt affinities with the plants and animals of the nature world more highly than it values their taxonomy or genetic manipulation. The very achievements that faith in science holds up as metaphors of true health it sees as metaphors of spiritual infection. Because the discourse of this faith is closer to the archaic languages of religion and philosophy than it is to the contemporary idiom of science, it is easily classified as the remnant of a prescientific mindset that is destined to be reformed as the evidence against it accumulates in the academies and eventually filters down to the masses. What seems to be happening is rather that the evidence in its favor is beginning to seep into the medical establishment itself.

The spectrum of beliefs marked off by allopathic medicine at one pole and wholistic medicine at the other seems to be more densely populated in the middle than at the extremes. Despite the growing interest in alternative medicines, it is caricature to think in terms of mass migrations from rationalism to spiritual aware-ness or from science to magic. For most people who live within reach of technologically advanced medicine, it is more a question of drifting a measured distance away from doctors and hospitals and standard medication in order to see what else might be out there. For such persons, the symbolism of the ICU is as ambivalent as is their faith in science.

All of this, I insist, cannot be a matter of indifference to Catholic moral reflection on health.

THE CATHOLIC MORAL COMPASS

The questions of medical ethics that occupy Catholics moralists are real problems that require careful attention. I am suggesting that there are more questions which, if ignored, bias the Catholic perspective in a morally unacceptable way. I will further suggest that the failure to widen the field to include these other questions can only further weaken the already seriously debilitated authority of the Catholic tradition. Nothing would be served by narrowing the focus of Catholicism's moral concerns to exclude the issues raised by technologically intensive scientific medicine, especially not in response to complaints that the medical profession can manage certain areas of health quite well on its own without the moralizing interference of nonspecialists. The problem is rather to determine where the needle points north on the Catholic moral compass.

Introducing the critique of present-day medicine and the viability of alternative medicines into the Catholic moral outlook is not meant to set up a choice between contradictories, but only to insure that the choice is not biased by tacit assumptions that run counter to Catholic tradition. The principal such assumption is the idea that the general advance of science and technology as such marks an irreversible stage of human civilization fated to cleanse the human spirit of its age-old addiction to superstition and magic. The role of Catholic moral reflection, accordingly, is to direct the use of the tools of science and technology as well as their institutional superstructures to the benefit of humanity and to resist abuses that offend the fundamental dignity of the human person. The spread of tools and institutions from a core of developed nations to the masses of underdeveloped peoples across the globe is therefore seen as a necessary and irrevocable fact of history. To belong to the present is to accept this fact; to belong to it as a Christian is to seek out its spiritual significance for the emerging global culture. The efforts of indigenous spiritualities and cultures to subsist apart from what is thought to be the very essence of human being—or at least to reserve the right to participate in the process at their own pace and in accord with their own values—are taken to be an affront to common sense and a deliberate disorientation from reality.

In a recent address, Cardinal Josef Ratzinger voiced these views in an explicit attack against the influx of alternative spiritualities into what he calls "universal Christian culture," an uncritical flood of primitive ideas that risk infecting the achievements of global, technological culture with "magic" and "cruelty":

> It is not only the case that the convergence of mankind towards a single community with a common life and destiny is unstoppable because such an inclination is grounded in man's essence, but also because the diffusion of technological civilization is *irrevocable*.... But since technology, like natural science, appears to be neutral, the thought suggests itself: Why not accept the achievements of the modern age while, however, at the same time keeping the indigenous religions? This seemingly so enlightened notion, however, does not work. For in reality modern civilization... alters the interpretation of the world at its base. It changes standards and behavior. The religious cosmos is *necessarily* moved by it.... The division of Western heritage into the useful, which one accepts, and the foreign, which one rejects, does not lead to the salvation of ancient cultures.[4]

As for the sacred texts of Asia's high religions (the address was delivered in Hong Kong), he welcomes them as serious resources in the battle against materialistic elements in Western technology, but not as a foundation for serious cultural alternatives. So not only Christianity but the achievements of Western Christian culture are to remain permanently on loan to the 200 million Christians of Asia, their own ancient cultures having outlived their usefulness for directing the relentless progress of globalization.

Fortunately for Catholicism, though perhaps unfortunately for its current leadership, the words of the Cardinal Prefect of the Congregation for the Doctrine of the Faith disobey the growing consensus of theologians around the world about the role of

Western culture in non-Western Christianity. I cite them here because they articulate the perspective within which Catholic moral reflection on scientific medicine tends to move when it comes to questions such as the allocation of ICU facilities for the terminally ill.

Once we broaden our view to take into account the way most of the world heals its sick and the broad range of spiritual meanings attending sickness and death, health and healing, it is by no means self-evident that moral questions surrounding the ICU require universal guidelines valid in principle for all health systems, let alone that the Western Catholic Church, in collaboration with the Western medical establishment, is in a position to provide them. The idea of solving local problems by global norms is every bit as culturally specific as the culture of high-tech medicine that generated these problems in the first place. The leap to universal relevance conceals a failure to ask if one culture of health— and a relatively recent one at that—should be allowed, even in a limited number of cases, to redefine for all of humanity what it means to resist sickness and die a good death. The side effects of scientific-technological medication reach far beyond the body parts it aims to repair, beyond the entire medical and pharmaceutical professions that administer the reparation. It is a kind of artificial culture produced in a controlled environment, immunized against threats to its homeostasis, and released on the open market for universal consumption. For Catholic moral reflection to serve the spread of this culture, even where it seems to be working according to design, without at the same time keeping these wider side effects in view is nothing short of a betrayal of its heritage.

It is not enough for Catholic morality to pose as a representative of worldwide culture. It must also proclaim as one collective voice the rich variety of vernacular cultures being swept along by historical tides not of their own choosing. The distinctively Catholic presence in creating guidelines for problems like high-level critical care should be to insist that they are not allowed to justify underlying biases inimical to the health of the masses of living persons who fall outside the purview of science's latest achievements. At some point, this will mean shifting the weight of its tradition and its resources towards protecting and encouraging alternative models of the healthy person and the medical vocation. Unlike medical science and the medical ethicists who serve its interests, Roman Catholicism cannot, without risking its soul, excuse itself from such questions on the grounds that there is no financial base to support alternatives, that the more "primitive" cultures of the world will have to succumb to the more "advanced" in matters of science and technology, or that the leaders of the world's "poorer" countries are poised to devour as much of the technology of the "richer" countries as they can. It cannot see things so simply and be faithful to the plurality of conditions in which its faith is lived around the world. Better the Church were criticized for being out of touch with who is winning the clash of civilizations than that it stand accused once again of having failed to speak for those whose voices were being drowned out by the current arrangements of power and wealth.

It may be objected that the moral authority of the Catholic Church will be weakened in proportion as it aligns itself with critics of the pillar institutions of the modern world and encourages alternatives. It seems more accurate to say that its authority is already being weakened because it does *not* do so. The time has come, it seems, to ask to what extent the teaching authority of Roman Catholic moralists can any longer expect to reach a substantial majority of its own believers, let alone the public at large, with its moral message. It is also time formally to decanonize the doctrine that there is no salvation for the Church outside the cultures of the world's ruling economies. No doubt there are certain moral issues today that by their nature override cultural differences, such as the reality of nuclear weaponry and industrial destruction of the environment. But when it comes to problems related to sickness and health, the Catholic Church cannot discard viable alternatives to the dominant models of medicine and at the same time retain its teaching authority towards those who pursue those alternatives. Readjusting the Catholic perspective on technologically intensive medical care requires an idea of Catholicity different from global uniformity and a view of death and suffering broader than the unconditional commitment to their alleviation. On both counts, the Catholic tradition is more likely to find stimulus in secular and primal spiritualities than in science and industry.

THE ILLOGIC OF UNIVERSAL GUIDELINES

The attempt to formulate norms to govern the operation of ICUs in the world's hospitals brings into clear relief the problem of grounding Catholic morality on universal principles that transcend cultures and institutions. Both logically and existentially, there are reasons for misgivings.

Regarding the logic of universal guidelines, a basic flaw has already been touched on: abstraction from the superstructure of the beliefs and institutions that generate the moral question at hand, and the side effects of that abstraction on cultures and individuals that do not share those beliefs and institutions. Clearly the universal applicability of ethical conclusions is seriously compromised if the very formulation of the question can be shown to exclude relevant moral data from the picture. In the case of traditional Catholic moral argumentation, this reduction of the moral field is supported by the appeal to "natural law" that in principle excludes the possibility of historical relativity from matters of ultimate concern. But when it comes to the application of universal moral principles to the use of technologically intensive medical equipment, the leap over time and place and culture to an objective order of truth and morality is more than an act of philosophical faith, principled or otherwise. It is a means of controlling the production of those values that support the "globalization" of particular ideas of sickness and health care. This is not a separate moral question, to be decided on other grounds. It is as essential a part of the ICU as the equipment, the technicians, and the cost-benefit analysis of the procedures.

In his philosophical essays Alfred North Whitehead was fond of chiding Western rationalism for what he formally called the "fallacy of misplaced concreteness."[5] By this he meant the tendency to attribute concrete reality to what are in fact mental abstractions. Plato fell into it when he forgot the abstractness of pure form and ascribed being to ideas; Aristotle, when he forgot the abstractness of simple individuality and argued for a primary substance; seventeenth-century science, when it assumed as concrete data the two abstractions of observing mind and observed matter. By and large, Western philosophy has accepted Whitehead's criticism as a commonplace (it had been so in the Buddhist philosophies of the East before the first philosophical idea had dawned in Plato's head), but fallacies with so long and noble a pedigree have a way of holding on. The idea of an objective moral order belonging to a natural law knowable in principle, though under no theoretical obligation to commit the fallacy, frequently does.

Universal moral principles are abstractions from culture, and as such always require reference to the relative values and aims of a culture to become concrete. Their universality is always mediated, never direct. To think otherwise is to read back into nature what has been drawn out of culture. We may call this sleight of logic "the fallacy of misplaced universality." By this I mean the tendency to attribute universal validity to what are in fact culturally specific values. In so doing, the *interests* of particular statements of universal morality are turned into *laws* of nature, and what would seem an anachronism to the philosophy of science is swallowed whole in ethics.

The history of colonialism provides ample evidence of how universal principles—particularly when reinforced by religious doctrine and technically superior equipment—can be evoked to disorganize one local culture and replace it with another. But even in the more enlightened, postcolonial age of the late twentieth century the fallacy survives in subtler though hardly less potent forms. On the face of it, there seems little to object to the establishing of general norms to insure distributive justice in critical medical care. On the one hand, we have the basic dignity of the human life; on the other, particular individuals of every shape and stripe, but all equal in their humanity. Hammer and anvil, these are, it would seem, tools enough with which to forge moral values of service to the whole of the human community. The only problem is, concrete human beings do not exist as particular examples of a general equation, and human life is nowhere to be found among the haphazard of items that make up the world. The particular and the universal are everywhere mediated by the specificity of human society, which cannot be abstracted from without forfeiting the concreteness of that which is being moralized about.

Without the specific, the relation of the individual to the community is merely a question of deciding the size of the relevant community to which one must answer. Surely the range of the community whose interests need to be taken into consideration when making decisions about appropriate medication is not irrelevant; it is crucial. But this does not exhaust the meaning of the specific. In such a scheme, communities—whether immediate family, the nation, the local township, or the whole community of nations—are aggregates of persons. The value of the culture that shapes both communities and individuals is ranked both below the value of the universal human and below the value of the individual person. As a result, not only is the cultural environment that shapes particular forms of rationalism and philosophic expression left out of the picture, so, too, is the value of protecting cultural pluriformity in the dissemination of Catholic moral values.

In questions related to medical care, to speak of the dignity of the human person *regardless* of culture, it seems to me, is to fall into a basic methodological error. To posit individual subjects and then lift the foundational ideas of human dignity and the sacredness of life up to the surface in order to cloak those individuals in "Catholic" moral value is to make a foundational idea perform a task it cannot perform—or at least cannot perform without falling into rationalism in the glum sense of the term. Not that religious values have nothing to do with universal human dignity, any more than medical science has nothing to do with universal human anatomy. But by identifying values as Catholic because of their universal applicability is to turn things inside out. If anything qualifies as Catholic, it cannot be simply in virtue of a universal judgment about a particular reality. It requires inclusion of the philosophically neglected category of the specific that necessarily mediates the relation between the universal and the particular.[6]

MORAL AND CULTURAL PLURALISM
AND THE MEANING OF HEALTH

This much can be extrapolated, it seems to me, from the logical fallacy of misplacing the universal. But recognition of the fallacy at work within the realm of faith and morals, and the determination to correct it, are neither prompted nor secured by contemplating the rules of logic. These are efforts of hindsight exerted in the attempt to appropriate more immediate, existential intuitions. If there are reasons to be suspicious of the true universality of moral guidelines governing equitable access to sophisticated medical technology, there are also reasons to question the idea that the foundations of these guidelines have been deduced from faith or reason. Insofar as they are of any consequence at all to moral choice, they need to be seen as interpretative paraphrases of faith and reason based on the awareness that violence is being done.

Appeals to principles such as the dignity of the human, the value of life, and the right to a good death are not, therefore, the *foundations* of conscience but an *expression* of conscience. The purpose of this expression is to alter certain habits of thought and action while maintaining continuity with others. The significance of these general principles—whether they be formulated in nonsectarian philosophies or in the scriptural and theological idiom of a particular religious tradition—lies in critically widening our perspective on immediate, living moral questions to prevent them from being expropriated by conventional social institutions. Their primary claim to authority over practical conscience is a function not of their provenance in faith or reason, nor of any innate transcendent truth in the formulation, but of the level of perception of the particular violence they address.[7]

The perception of violence that present-day Catholic thinking brings to problems of medical care is no longer restricted to the treatment of the individual. It includes the social consequences of the institutions that provide the treatment. Whereas the imagination of those dependent on access to the latest medical technology seems by and large to have resigned itself to the institutional contours that define the pursuit and practice of modern medicine, and provide a framework for dealing with particular issues, there is something in the Catholic vision that feels cramped and uncomfortable in these same circumstances. Attempts to work within the existing institutionalization of medicine in order to try to rein in its excesses and protect it from injustice and oppression, for all the enthusiasm with which these attempts are made, yet leave a residue of dissatisfaction. I am not talking about the accusations of inadequacy, incompetence, and ineffectiveness that those at the cutting edge of science often use to bleed the enthusiastic temper of its less-informed critics. I mean something more in the nature of an uneasy sense of those structural disorders that have been excluded from the picture. True, the suspicion of structural disorder is a distinctively contemporary preoccupation that religious ethics has inherited from secular social criticism, but its place in Catholic self-understanding has been secured by a generation of theological reflection. That said, it is still engaged in a tug-of-war with elements in the tradition that persist in isolating the health and salvation of the individual from the reality of social violence.

The allegiance to technological civilization begs the question of cultural pluralism by assuming that a basic, uniform, global cultural form pedals in tandem with the tools of modern Western society and its view of the cosmos. On such an assumption, the business of organized religion is to insure that the whole package—the tools and the cultural forms in which they are embedded—does not infringe on basic human rights but enhances the quality of life. This very identification of technological civilization with its Western form introduces a colonial dimension to any Catholic morality that supports it without serious question. The accomplishments of modern medicine do not as such justify the cultural and institutional form in which those tools have been embedded. Nor do they gainsay the possibility that the aims of medicine might as well be served if wedded to radically other forms of civilization with histories different from those of Europe and the United States.

Mere dismantling of the offending structures and a simple transfer of the tools of modern medicine into the hands of societies that did not participate in their invention and development is naïve. Even were the transfer to succeed, it would likely do so only by reimporting the structures in a subtler form. At the same time, the hope of awakening moral conscience for the totality of the structure in all those on whom the structure leans for its existence is unrealistic. Quantitatively speaking, most of our sin, like most of our virtue, takes the form of cliché. Most of the common courtesies of everyday life that make human intercourse pleasant, as well as most of the prejudices that keep us at a distance from one another, are the result of unwitting force of habit. Important as consciousness of sin and willfully cultivated virtue are, they are no match for the power of structural evil. But to see our institutions as no more than necessary evils, doomed one day to fall prey to their own darker nature, is a caricature of culture itself. They must be seen as experiments with belief in our ideals, the ultimate goodness of our humanity, experiments that can only be radically corrected by the encounter with other, alternative experiments. Without wishing to deny the reality of the issues that surround critical care at the edge of medical science today, it does not seem fair to exclude alternative models or to assume that they will all embrace the same questions with the same sense of "emergency" that surrounds the dominant health culture.

Again, it is not a question of asking the Church to divest itself outright of Western civilization. Rather, insofar as the Church is determined to participate in the production of moral guidelines to lead the technological civilization of the West, let it just as far participate in supporting alternative forms for wielding the technology. The imbalance of resources devoted to the former amounts to a denial of the latter. In such circumstances, every step taken to Catholicize health ends up catholicizing a culture of health that for vast numbers of the human family is still parochial and foreign.

Now for all the trust we have in the pillar institutions of contemporary society, our understanding of the way they transform our perception of the world is still meager in comparison with our understanding of how to manage them at home and export them abroad. Clearly we are caught in a bind. On the one hand, we look with alarm at what transformations in schools, hospitals, agriculture, financial markets, mass transport, and even organized religion have done to traditional values in the societies where progress has been most marked. On the other, our dependency on these institutions prevents us from standing in the way of their continued expansion.

To make matters worse, the damage a particular society can sustain through the unchecked development of its central institutions is compounded and accelerated, not checked and balanced, when the cultural diversity of societies around the world is made subservient to the mechanisms of a globally interconnected world. Like the media for the exchange of information which parade an unlimited variety on the surface even as they canonize an underlying structural uniformity, the internationalizing of those institutions to which we entrust the major dimensions of our lives advances steadily away from supporting the cultures they were intended to uphold and enhance. The plurality of cultures cannot survive unconnected from one another, and yet their connections seem to pressure them into a uniformity that trivializes the meaning of pluralism.

As with a greater concentration of power, a greater accumulation of information and perfection of technique are no guarantee that an institution will not promote the frustration of its original purpose. In this regard, the poverty of insight into alternative ideas of health—not just alternative forms of medicine or alternative forms of organized care, but alternative ideas of what it means to be healthy and of what are the limits of resisting suffering and death—seems to be in inverse proportion to the wealth of knowledge about the latest advances in medical science. From the ordained experts of the health industry to the functionaries who administer it to the recipients who have come to depend on it, the measure of physical well-being is simply assumed to be as transcultural and universal as the periodic table of the elements. Within the course of our own lifetimes, traditional ideas of health around the world have been redefined as a sickness, the cure to which lies in the hands of those with knowledge and equipment so far superior that it seems folly to resist. Evidence that the quality of human life has been enhanced as a result, even where the dominant model of health has taken strongest root, is flimsy.

Data gathered over the past two decades on iatrogenic illness—namely, diseases contracted through the very services that set out to cure disease—seem to have had a certain sobering effect on the health industries. But the idea that "health" itself may be an iatrogenic malady specific to certain societies and inflicted on others is all but unthinkable. Modern medical care is too much part of the "package" of modern life to be isolated as a particular colonial construct that economically backward cultures are free to take or leave. Intensive care, the exchange of organs, and other high-order surgery are no longer viewed as luxury items but as the legitimate right of all people everywhere. Despite the complexities involved in providing such care and the economic superstructure needed to sustain the equipment and personnel, it has come to be seen as a basic resource of all human culture. Together with food, clothing, shelter, literacy, and work, it has become one more item on the moralist's agenda for distributive justice.

There is no denying the moral dilemma for those who stand at arm's length from the very best equipment medical science has to offer and have to decide where to apply it and where to withhold application. Nor is there any doubt that such decisions require carefully reflected norms and guidelines. It is quite another thing, however, to allow such examples to beg the question of whether the dilemma and its ethical resolution, together with the whole medical culture to which they are specific, should simply be accepted as the inevitable fate of all people everywhere. Policing the morals of a civilization where the poor cannot get the same care as the wealthy, and where the financing of health has made higher health care impossible without dedicating a sizable part of one's income to insurance against the harsh realities of hospital costs, is work enough without bothering about the more basic question of whether the goal of providing everyone everywhere with the same high level of care is a worthwhile goal at all.

In a word, the thoughts of a certain portion of the human community about health and longevity have become the form of all thought about health, and the rich plurality of beliefs, rituals, and even superstitions surrounding sickness and death has lost its power to the imperial myth of modern health care. Like all empires, it is a specificity masquerading as a universal. And like all myth, it has seeped into common sense so that it is virtually transparent to opinion polls and ordinary decision-making. In matters of the gravest consequence, the distinction between what is indigenous and what imported has become irrelevant. One of the richest sources of human diversity—the practices and attitudes surrounding death and illness—has been sacrificed to a worldwide campaign for uniformity regarding what it means to be well and what it means to die.[8]

The very fact of insisting on the inclusion of "alternative" models to health care in the field of discussions about medical ethics entails some degree of cultural anarchy (in the sense of breaking with the *archaí,* or ruling principles). Awareness of the threat of structural violence in the medical professions demands that this be done. Of all the great religious traditions of the world today, perhaps none is as well-prepared, as missiologically alert, and as self-reflective as the Catholic Church to commit the weight of its tradition to meet this demand.

Not only those who continue to identify themselves with one or the other form of organized religion, but also the greater part of those who run the organizations trying to keep them there, are relying more and more on the moral sensitivities of those outside of religion for guidance. The fact is, the major moral enthusiasms of the age—for the preservation of the natural world, for the eradication of slave labor, for freedom of thought and expression, for the protection of minorities against the democratic majority— were neither inspired by organized religion in the first place nor have they depended on organized religion for their vitality. Quite the opposite, it is only by tapping into this enthusiasm that organized religion can maintain any moral authority at all towards the contemporary world. I do not see the retreat of the Catholic Church from the construction of a global, universal world order as submission to the rising black tide of secular paganism, but as a call to purge Catholic tradition of its colonial vestiges and to turn the considerable resources of the Church towards the preservation of cultural pluralism and alternative models of social order. In the context of moral reflection on health and medication, the Catholic viewpoint would see conventional institutions, however strong or however weak they happen to be in a particular setting, as more like local churches than like local branches of an ecclesiastical multinational. The difference is not trivial. In the former, the question is always how to wrestle what is best from vernacular culture and at the same time pry open its conscience towards the world outside of it; in the latter, the question is rather how to maintain uniformity in essential modes of thought and behavior while allowing for variation in the accidentals.

Before committing itself to the formulation of universal guidelines for access to critical care, the Catholic moralist must at least take into account two interrelated facts. First, the health-care systems of most of the world are likely to embrace a code of universal principles governing the application of critical care only if they perceive it as one of the conditions for receiving the latest medical technology or for being allowed access to it as the need arises. Once they have the technology firmly in their own grasp, the authority of the principles is exhausted. Second, the truly Catholic perspective on health always opens up a horizon wider than the medical complexes of Europe and the United States; these latter never represent more than a minority opinion. We cannot, as Catholics, simply make principles based on one set of cultural forms and then ask others to adjust them to their own conditions. This is what I mean by claiming the ethical imagination is constrained to a perspective that deprives the Catholic tradition of its fullest contribution.

At all levels—of universal principles, of institutional structure, and of individual spirituality—the Catholic moral imagination needs a kind of cultural refund from the advances of the medical industry. It is an industry that brings to the medication of the individual patient the authority of the knowledge, the facilities, and the organization it has at its command. As such it is a kind of new Church universal whose values justify themselves in statistical effectiveness of healing illness. But it is not, and can never be, a *Catholic* Church. To allow the industry to pose the questions in its own terms, and not radically to overturn them in the light of religious tradition, is not only un-Catholic, it is irreligious. This is how I understand the summons to join you in discussing the problem of allocating critical care in the light of Catholic belief.

NOTES

[1] D. M. Eisenberg et al, "Trends in Alternative Medicine Use in the United States, 1990-1997," *The Journal of the American Medical Association* 280 (1998): 15690-775.

[2] According to M. S. Wetzel et al, "Courses Involving Complementary and Alternative Medicine at US Medical Schools," *The Journal of the American Medical Association* 280 (1998): 784–7, the majority of medical schools in the United States now offer courses on alternative medicine.

[3] Rustom Roy, "Whole Person Healing." Keynote address to the Third Yōkō

Civilization International Congress, Takayama, Japan, 18 August 1999.

[4] J. Ratzinger, "Christian Faith and the Challenge of Cultures," *Origins* 24 (1955): 683–4. Emphasis added.

[5] A. N. Whitehead, *Science and the Modern World* (New York: Macmillan, 1925), 52–6.

[6] One of the most sophisticated philosophical arguments, posed in the language and sources of Western philosophy, on this neglect of the specific is to be found in the works of the Japanese philosopher Tanabe Hajime. His idea is that the specificity carried by culture mediates between universal humanity and the individual person, providing not only values and the parameters of reason, but also the fund of ethnocentric thinking and irrationality that feeds isolationism and colonialism alike. I have outlined this in several essays, including "Tanabe's Logic of the Specific and the Spirit of Nationalism," James W. Heisig and John C. Maraldo, eds., *Rude Awakenings: Zen, the Kyoto School, and the Question of Nationalism* (Honolulu: University of Hawaii Press, 1995): 255–88; and "Tanabe's Logic of the Specific and the Critique of the Global Village," *The Eastern Buddhist* 28/2 (1995): 198–224.

[7] In this regard, see Carlos Eduardo Maldonado, *Human Rights, Solidarity, and Subsidiarity: Essays toward a Social Ontology* (Washington, D.C.: Council for Research in Values and Philosophy, 1997), 9–28.

[8] See Prem Chandran John, "The Millennial Migraine: Health Care and the Poor in the 21st Century," Nagoya University, Graduate School of International Development.

The Recovery of the Senses
Against the Asceticisms of the Age

When Ivan Illich visited us at the Nanzan Institute in 1986, we talked about inviting a group of people to discuss the ways in which the body has been fragmented and the senses expropriated by the institutions of modern society. At the time, Wilfred Cantwell Smith was staying with us, and discussions with him centered around his work on the "Song of Songs" and the way in which its reading throughout the history of Christianity has crystallized radically different attitudes towards the role of the body.

Although our planned seminar never materialized, in anticipation that it would, I decided to delve into another scriptural tradition, that of the gnostics, in search of a link between the devaluation of the senses that results from an expressly religious worldview and one that results from an expressly irreligious one. The closer I came to the texts themselves, the further I moved away from the received opinion about gnosticism's singleminded bias against the body and from the connections I had hoped to draw.

Some years later, in 1993, I was asked to prepare a paper for the annual meeting of the Japan Society for Buddhist-Christian Studies in Kyoto. To complement Buddhist presentations on Yogācāra theories of perception and insight, I was to address the role of religious experience in reawakening the senses.

For religions working in dialogue such as Buddhism and Christianity, waking up to the routine "asceticisms" of industrialized civilization and working together for the rehabilitation of the senses seemed to me one measure of

*their ongoing mutual transformation. As a common forum
on which Buddhism and Christianity could meet to exam-
ine the question, I settled on the gnostic Gospel of Thomas.
It seemed to me then, and still does, that there are many
points in Gnosticism that bridge the two religious ways.
While historical research into the influence of Buddhist
ideas on gnostic thought is still very incomplete, the texts
themselves offer a way of paraphrasing any number of issues
central to the interrreligious encounter today, among them
the particular neglect of the body that classical religions
have contracted from industrialized civilization.*

*The pages that follow are an attempt to paraphrase a
contemporary question in the context of a commentary on
key passages from that gnostic Gospel. At a future date I
hope to write a longer commentary on the text in its
entirety.*

Originally published as「五感の快復──時代の禁欲主義
に抗して」『慈悲・身体・智慧』[Compassion, Body,
Wisdom], ed. by the Sophia University Institute for Oriental
Religions (Tokyo: Shunjūsha, 1994): 71–108. The English
translation subsequently appeared in the *Journal of Ecumenical Studies* 33/2 (Spring 1996): 216–37.

THERE IS AN ancient Buddhist story about a man who is being chased by a pair of rogue elephants. Fearing for his life, he climbs into a well and grabs hold of a vine growing out of the wall, just beyond reach of the tusks of the pursuing beasts. He notices two mice, one white and one black, gnawing at the vine. Meantime four poisonous snakes begin climbing up the walls towards him and three fierce, fire-breathing dragons lie menacingly at the bottom of the well. As the man looks up he chances to notice a few drops of honey clinging to the vine. He pauses to savor their sweetness and in that instant is freed from all his fear.[1]

Death's pursuit of life, the fact that we are born prey to time and must—against our deepest will—one day yield to it, is among the foundational insights of religion. What distinguishes the orientation of religions one from another is the interpretative framework of symbols, ideas, and practices drawn about this pessimistic wisdom in order to turn it into an affirmation of life. In the parable just cited, the Buddhist context is clarified by an interpolated commentary: The two elephants are the wheel of *saṃsāra*, of coming-to-be and passing-away. The well is the impermanence of our human state. The black and white mice are the moon and the sun which gnaw away at life (the vine) from dawn to dusk, day in and day out. The venomous snakes represent the four elements (earth, fire, water, wind) of which all things are made but which also work incessantly to unmake all things. The three dragons are the three poisons of covetousness, anger, and folly. Together they represent a total and all-encompassing threat that is suspended by a simple satisfaction of the senses (the taste of honey).[2]

The attractiveness of this image of a man savoring a few drops of honey as his life draws to a close seems to lie in its implicit counsel that we, in the fullness of life, "let go" of our attachment to ordinary ideas about life and death, that we surrender ourselves entirely to the moment. The enjoyment of the honey signifies a liberation from the duty of making rational sense of the things of life, but its significance does not stop there. It seems to announce a liberation from the very preoccupation with liberation. As long as the fugitive is absorbed in the taste of honey, he is free of the question of his own salvation, and at the same time he is saved as much as any living being can be saved. The proof of salvation here lies not in insight but in absorption in a simple filling up of the senses—in this case a satisfying one—that breaks through the obsession with insight.

This idea of salvation through "salvation from salvation," though not always the immediate focus of Buddhist thought and practice, seems to me to reach deep into the ground of religious experience where the roots of Buddhism and Christianity are tangled indistinguishably. I would like to suggest that this simple but radical truth be turned to the question of recovering the senses from the expropriation of the asceticisms obliged on us by the age in which we live. The idea that religious insight and experience should change not only the way the inner eye sees the things of life and the life of virtue that this insight informs, but also the way the body senses the world bears particular importance for us. If food tastes the same, if fragrances smell the same, if surfaces feel the same as they did before, then the salvific value of insight and virtue are suspect. In the same way that consistency with received tradition is taken as a measure of religious truth, or *orthodoxy*, the embodiment of tradition in the moral choices of life is understood to be a measure of religious action, or *orthopraxis*. But these two—right thinking and right action—are incomplete without some measure of the true liberation of the senses, an *orthoaesthesis*.

There is a story in the *Jātaka* that illustrates the connection between praxis and aesthesis in early Buddhist tradition. It is said that a certain king went out in search of a Bodhisattva to tell him his faults that he might reign more justly. The sage offered him a ripe fig. The king ate it and was surprised that the fig was so sweet. The ascetic tells him, "The king now exercises his rule with justice and equity. That is why it is so sweet." "In the reign of an unjust king," asked the king, "does it lose its sweetness?" "It does," replied the Bodhisattva. "In the time of unjust kings, oil, honey, molasses and the like, as well as wild roots and fruits, lose their sweetness and flavor. But when the rules are just, these things become sweet and full of flavor." At this the king returned home and, to test the advice of the Bodhisattva, began to rule unjustly. He found that indeed the fruit tasted bitter, while after he began to rule justly again, the fruit regained its sweetness.[3]

The recovery of the fig's sweetness is not a mere metaphor for the recovery of moral virtue, any more than moral action is a mere metaphor for an inward state. Both are sacramental confirmations of religious experience, outward signs of an inward grace. If true justice is the embodiment of enlightened insight, so is true savoring. The man clinging to a vine and enjoying the sweetness of the honey is confirming his awareness as much as the king who acts in a moral and upright manner.

In the poet Aśvaghoṣa's account of the Buddha's life in the *Buddhacarita*, the sequence is reversed: the recovery of the senses from deprivation precedes the decision to undertake a life of compassionate action in the world. This in turn highlights an interesting contrast between the initial resolve of the young Prince Gotama and what he ends up discovering. On deciding to leave home for homelessness, Gotama borrows the sword of his friend Chandaka, cuts off his hair and tosses it into the lake, and announces his intention: "Either I will extinguish old age and death, and then you shall quickly see me again; or I will go to perdition, because my strength has failed me and I could not achieve my purpose." At this he departs into the forest for a life of self-torture, hoping thereby to reach his goal. At each stage of his disenchantment from the self-preoccupation of his initial resolve and its rigorous asceticism, culminating in full enlightenment as a

Buddha, insight is accompanied by a reaction in nature. The moon comes out. Sweet-smelling flowers fall from the skies. Dawn breaks. The earth trembles like a woman drunk with wine. Rain falls from a cloudless sky.

To understand the poet's purpose, it is not enough to see the Buddha as a universal sage whose impact extends throughout the heavens and the earth. The reactions of nature suggest that in awakening Gotama has finally "come to his senses." Only then does he decide to become a teacher and "beat the drum of the undying Dharma to a world grown dark."[4] Salvation is not for disembodied, anesthetized minds but for "sentient beings," and their salvation cannot but include a rehabilitation of lost sentience. It is not without reason that the most ancient records of the Buddha's teaching depict the person as anything but a disembodied spirit destined for enlightenment. The following is typical:

> These four are the foodstuffs, ye bhikkus, which sustain the creatures that are born, and benefit the creatures that seek rebirth. The first is edible food, coarse or fine; touch is the second; the thinking capacity of the mind is the third; and the fourth is consciousness.[5]

The Buddha did not in fact erase life and death from the context of ordinary life. Life goes on, and with it death and old age and sickness. No amount of insight can stop the wheel this side of death. If awakened insight sees this and this alone, it is not yet "saved" from the wheel. Surely salvation also means that the things of life look and taste and smell and feel and sound differently to one who has seen through the impermanence of all things—not necessarily more painful or more pleasant, but certainly more intense.

There is a vast difference between the senses that Gotama represses in order to open the mind's eye and the senses that are released again once he has seen. To the awakened, the moon regains its luster and flowers their fragrance, the rain is refreshing, the earth comes alive. Without the drops of honey, enlightenment is no more than being trapped in an old well with danger on all sides. If the darkness of ignorance clouds the senses the more one tries to satisfy them, the light of insight should revitalize the senses and make them more alert to experience. If not, enlightened insight is no more than a shifting of the boundaries between the rational and the irrational.

I

The Christian mystical tradition is not without its own expression of the recovery of the senses as a kind of "proof" of religious experience. The Flemish "love mystics" of the thirteenth century are rich in examples. In this regard they stand in marked contrast to the Rhineland mystics, for whom the perceptions of "sight" provided primary metaphors for mystical "insight" and directed attention to the soul as a dry spark in the desert air, to the pure light of godhead that detaches us from space and time and corporeality.[6] Even when we see a figure like Eckhart stressing the importance of making contemplation subservient to deeds, the locus of religious transformation remains the soul, which the human has in common with the angels, "those noblest of all creatures, who are purely spiritual and have nothing corporeal."[7] It is other with the Flemish mystics, where spiritual insight and language seem often to serve as metaphors for the transfiguration that has taken place in the corporeal realms of touch and taste.

The visions of the thirteenth-century mystic known to history as Hadewijch are instructive in this regard. Towards the end of the twelfth century a movement for a new style of life had begun among women belonging to the nobility or upper-class families. Rejecting the sheltered cloister of castle and convent alike, these "beguines" as they were called practiced a common life of simplicity and meditation. Hadewijch belonged to one such community, though her attempts to integrate the ideals of romantic love with religious experience eventually led to her banishment.

The poet Gottfried, whose medieval romance *Tristan and Isolde* was a model of the suspicion and excitement that surrounded the open revival of courtship, suggests that the same nourishment that the believer finds in the bread of the eucharist is given to the noble soul through erotic experience.[8] For Hadewijch, it was not a question of opting for one or the other but of coming to a "union with full possession" wherein the two are one. The seventh of her reported visions is a clear example.

During the early morning prayer of Matins on Pentecost Sunday, she feels herself overcome by an intense expectation at which "my heart and my veins and all my limbs trembled and quivered with eager desire." An eagle appears to her and tells her to get ready if she wants oneness. The eagle then addresses Christ, saying: "Now show your great power to unite your oneness in the manner of union with full possession." Christ comes down from the cross above the altar three times to Hadewijch, who is kneeling at her place in the chapel.

The first time he appears as a child of three years old, offering her the bread and wine of communion. Next he appears as a grown man, giving himself first in religious ritual form, and then in full physical union.

> With that he came in the form and clothing of a Man, as he was on the day when he gave us his Body for the first time; looking like a Human Being and a Man, wonderful, and beautiful, and with glorious face, he came to me as humbly as anyone who wholly belongs to another. Then he gave himself to me in the shape of the Sacrament, in its outward form, as the custom is; and then he gave me to drink from the chalice, in form and taste, as the custom is.
>
> After that he came himself to me, took me entirely in his arms, and pressed me to him; and with all my members felt his in full felicity, in accordance with the desire of my heart and my humanity. So I was outwardly satisfied and fully transported.

As her ecstasy abates, the original sensations return one by one, though in different form. The hallucination does not end in William Blake's ephemeral "cleansing of the doors of perception," but gives new life to old habits.

> Also then, for a short while, I had the strength to bear this; but soon, after a short time, I lost that manly beauty outwardly in the

sight of his form. I saw him completely come to naught and so far and all at once dissolve that I could no longer recognize or perceive him outside me, and I could no longer distinguish him within me. Then it was to me as if we were one without difference. It was thus: outwardly, to see, taste, and feel, as one can outwardly taste, see, and feel in the reception of the outward Sacrament. So can the Beloved, with the loved one, each wholly receive the other in full satisfaction of the sight, the hearing, and the passing away of the one in the other.[9]

Hadewijch's recovery of the senses in the reception of holy communion is a striking instance of how religious experience can transform the normal experience of the senses. The transportation beyond the sensing self, so that "nothing any longer remained in me of myself," is as far from hedonism as it is from moral conscience. It is as if the natural overflow of grace and insight into the exercise of compassion or love in human society just as naturally flows on into the reawakening of senses mortified by routine and conventional expectations.For recovery implies that something genuine has been lost; and recovery in religious experience suggests further that what has been lost is the result not only of ignorance and sin, but of the blindness of insight and spiritual love to the deprivations of the body.

II

Moral and religious leaders concerned with the quality of human life often speak of the consumer society as a colossal beast with a ravenous appetite for goods and services on the one end, and on the other, a shameless disregard for dumping its waste. The idea of looking at a human society as a corpus that feeds on the earth and either competes or cooperates with other human societies for available resources has been in circulation for no more than a hundred years. By the dawn of the new century, this view of human societies as moral entities accountable to each other and to conventional ideas of the natural world will probably qualify as common sense.

The moral outrage directed against consumer society is strongest among those who belong to societies that in fact do the most consuming. Technologically simpler, less consumptive societies are more readily applauded by those who have in excess of what they need than by those who need in excess of what they have. By and large, those who have come to think of themselves as "underdeveloped" find the patterns of consumption of the "developed" far more appealing than the ideas of the small minority who question the foundations of the distinction between rich and poor. The idea of returning to E. F. Schumacher's "appropriate technologies" or Ivan Illich's "subsistence economies" has taken stronger hold among the beneficiaries of development than among its victims. In this sense, the gap between people who think of themselves as over-consumptive and those who think of themselves as under-consumptive is strengthened by the very ideas that purport to close it.

The irony is as old as civilization itself: catholicizing modes of thought are so often radically parochial to the time and place that shaped them. In the case of civilization at the end of the twentieth century, the transformation of insights into universal archetypes is glossed over by a tacit faith in the objectivity of scientific data and the expertise of those who gather it. There is no need to ignore, for instance, the accumulation of *data* about irreparable damage done to the biosphere and the atmosphere of planet earth to have a second look at the way in which they function as *capta* of particular cultures empowered to use them for their own agenda.

Put another way, the metaphor of the consumer society, compelling as it is for individual consumers who want to break free to believe something other than what they have been taught to believe, casts its own shadow of tacit assumptions. It is in this shadow that I would like to try to look for a way out of the unrepentant moralizing of those who have seen the light. In particular, I propose that we consider the way in which modern habits of consumption amount to a collective self-mortification that ranks among the most outrageous excesses of the ascetical traditions East and West. In shifting the focus away from the gluttony of the corporate beast to the deprivation of the individual citizen, there is I believe some hope of reclaiming a higher measure of satisfaction without first having to secure the right to police the conscience of the world in the name of universal principles bred under the jurisdiction of scientific technique.

The asceticism of contemporary life is at best a caricature of its classical religious counterpart, and that for one simple reason: its practice is by and large unaware. The intensity of the isolation, mortification of the appetites, and frigidity of the senses exacted from those who choose to live at the core of the civilized world is better measured by the amount of drowsiness these things induce than by any waking afflictions. Far from the ideal of a sacramental discipline, the asceticism of everyday is no more than a submission to routine, an outward sign of an inward barrenness.

The symptoms of the deprivation are everywhere. Attentiveness to the immediacy of conversation, of keeping company with another through the exchange of word and gesture, deteriorates in proportion as the amount of spoken words and visual images received through the one-way traffic of mass media. The love of learning is corralled into a love of grading, where it is repressed and debilitated by objective standards that dishonor the education of the senses as beyond the standards of certification. Those who pursue learning outside of the channels are "degraded." The taste for fresh, unprocessed food is forfeited in favor of what is more affordable. Long hours spent indoors under conditions of artificial light and heat weaken bodily alertness to the change of the seasons. Artifically concocted fragrances redefine a range of natural odors as disagreeable or unhealthy. The time-saving machinery that extends the capacity of the bodily limbs and organs slowly amputates the basic rudiments of grace and rhythm from the workplace and redefines it as a proprium of the sports arena or gymnasium. The identification of work with wage-earnings, which has made it acceptable to forfeit more basic satisfactions of productive work in order to provide oneself and one's dependents with the necessities of life, supports this and other forms of reification of the body as an object of specialization. In effect, submission to employment full-time on these terms amounts to a mandatory renunciation of the full employment of the individual worker. Or again, as music and song become identified with the mechanical apparatus to reproduce them, the pleasure of live performance becomes a luxury entrusted to the care of professionals and to be enjoyed, again, only as far as one can afford it.

The same deprivations pass over into our ability to judge the quality of things and people. We purchase things by labels which certify that someone else has checked their quality or utility. No matter how often we are deceived, we simply choose other labels to confide in until we are let down. Certificates of higher education perform much the same function for deciding on an individual's intelligence or capacity for performing a service. Fail us though it may, our trust in the standards of measurement is all but immune to disenchantment. For want of being consulted, common sense and experience lose their authority.

In flattering our appetites, or trying to survive those of others, we are often simply anesthetizing them. The more superhuman the pace at which one is shuttled about in mechanical devices, the more the goods and services one piles up, the more the spirit drags itself about in a kind of sleepwalk. This is what I mean by the asceticisms of the age.

The environment that supports this charade is not restricted to the industries that feed on it. As more and more people are beginning to realize, it is also a state of mind—and one *within reach of individual virtue*. The choice against deprivation need not wait for the reform of social structures. It can inaugurate a simple revolution in the quest for a simpler, more sufficient, more satisfying way of life. Translated directly into concrete behavior, such a revolution may seem to be more than the exchange of less painful, unconscious ascesis for a more painful conscious one. I therefore think it important to stress the positive recovery of the senses as a measure of the relief from unhappiness.

In order to imagine as clearly as possible an alternative to the present exercise of the senses, one needs first to awaken from the spell of deprivation—to close one's eyes, give them a good rub, and open them again to see the way in which accustomed delights work a compulsory asceticism on our native appetite for happiness. It is a mistake from the start to think of such re-visioning of the everyday world as a kind of simple preparatory step up a steep mountain to higher consciousness. It is always and ever the point of return. The savoring of the immediacy of everyday life remains the measure of insight, but its recovery is as arduous and demanding as surrender to habit is relaxed and self-indulgent. In this sense, the renunciation of ascetical consumption requires a model of discipline, some image of restoration that can serve as a kind of "guiding fiction" along the way. This, it seems to me, is a neglected moral challenge that Christianity and Buddhism share together in our time.

III

In taking up a subject as far-reaching as the restoration of the senses, the demand for a workable alternative social structure—for in the end nothing less will do—is sure to arise. I have no such scheme at hand, and am in fact rather skeptical of generating it in our present condition. It seems to me work enough to try to see as clearly as we can where the course of events has landed us, and to hold our predicament up to the light of the best ideals the past has to offer for the art of living. This is what I understand it to mean for a religious tradition to "hold a text sacred," which is different from simply revering a deposit of seamless, trans-epochal truth. It is not as a torch in the darkness that we turn to such texts, but as the dim but inviting glow of a hearth around which to gather and think through untimely thoughts.

A patient reading of the Gospel of Thomas, a first-century Coptic manuscript discovered in 1945 in an ancient library at Nag Hammadi in Egypt, has convinced me that just such a sacred quality peeks out from behind the difficult images and alien idiom in which it expresses the relation between enlightened insight and the senses. Enough has been written on the text to spare me the burden of going into too much detail on its origins, composition, or translation.[10] The doctrine of the senses is something else again and requires a rather severe reorientation to recover.

Modern commentators have had a rather easy time of finding familiar notions of "the self" in the text by turning reflexive personal pronouns into nouns. The process of turning *self-knowledge*, *self-realization*, and *self-discovery* into knowledge, discovery, and realization *of the Self* is so natural—and has been to the West ever since Fichte gave modern philosophy the notion of *das Ich*—as to be all but transparent to today's reader. And from there it is but a short step to understand the *gnosis* as endorsing a primitive form of depth-psychology.[11] The rich connections with Eastern philosophies, though not easy to establish historically, support the effort. This would not matter so much did it not ultimately eclipse a quite different, and I believe important, notion of the self to be found in the Gospel of Thomas.

The most convincing reason for the lapse of conscience in psychologizing the text is, of course, the obvious influence of Gnosticism, for which both body and soul were apparently demiurgic creations that need to be overcome in the name of a higher "inner life." The focus of its asceticism was not simply body, but a body-mind state of being that needed to be cast away like old garments in order that the original inner nature which they obscure can come to life.

Lacking the richer terminology of Eastern languages, Greek writers and translators had to make do with substituting uncommon usages to speak of the other-worldly center to human being. The natural life of the person was referred to as *psychic* and the supernatural as *pneumatic* (a usage adopted also in St. Paul). And yet, even if one grants with Hans Jonas that "this transcendent inner principle in man and the supreme concern about its destiny is the very center of gnostic religion," this does not justify identifying it as an individual property. Just as Plato's and Augustine's inner soul represented a step beyond individual personality to a "God within," so did the Mandean notion of "Mana" establish an identity between this inner principle and the godhead.[12] The notion of an archetypal individuum waiting in the unconscious like a seed for the bright sun of consciousness to release its power and transform the person into a harmonious, unified Self required a rather more modern understanding of the individual.

But more important still for the Gospel of Thomas and what it has to say about the senses, the "influence" of gnostic ideas of body and soul was not received uncritically by Christian writers of the early centuries. As is well known, were it not for the critical resistance of Irenaeus, Hippolytus, and Epiphanius against gnostic teachings, we would have too little information to put together a clear picture of just what Gnosticism was. But this does not justify the assumption that those who were most affected by it were in the same measure uncritical of what they were taking in. In principle, scholars are agreed that this took place.[13] In fact, little evidence has been advanced to show just how and where.

Fidelity to the canonical gospels was not a primary concern in this process, but neither was fidelity to any particular gnostic sect. Scholars continue to speculate on the possibility that the Gospel of Thomas had access to sources that pre-date the gospels as we know them today, but there is agreement that it was read in a variety of gnostic and Manichean circles.[14] Not only the dating of its composition around the latter part of the second century, but its use by the Christian communities in eastern Syria already alerts us to a selective appropriation of both Christian and gnostic sources.

Leaving aside the question of how far the general gnostic distemper towards the world of the senses might have been alleviated by Christian influence, the Gospel of Thomas is remarkable for its freedom from contagion. Only a deliberate disinfection of the gnostic vision could account for the absence of so central an element. In the case of the Gospel of Thomas this is brought about by enlisting Gnosticism's own metaphors for the counter-purpose of a resurrectional theology. In other words, just as the gnostic teachings inverted the meaning of Christian doctrine in order to provide "food for the fed-up" among the Christian communities,[15] so does the Gospel of Thomas turn the tables by using gnostic images to preach a liberation from the repression of the senses.

It is not at all clear that the influence of gnostic "asceticism" on Christian thought always took the form of a simple repression of the senses. (Does not the Gospel of Philip, a heavily gnostic work dating from a century later than the Gospel of Thomas, give us the lurid scenes of Jesus offending the disciples by kissing Mary Magdalene on the mouth?) Gnosticism itself was not cut of a single cloth regarding the role of the senses, and there is no evidence that Christian writers favored the more disembodied, spiritualizing gnostic tendencies. The *florilegium* of the Gospel of Thomas, as I hope to show, is no exception.

IV

From the start, the aphoristic and recondite style of the Gospel of Thomas disapproves of rational organization of its ideas. At the same time, many of the sayings, if not most, are linked according to a number of main themes, reiterated to unify the whole.[16] The treatment of the senses, although an integral part of the text, is not one of those main themes but can only be gleaned along the way by someone predisposed to look for it. Whether that disposition illumines or dims the reading of the Gospel of Thomas is for others to say. Meantime, as I record my own reading, economy obliges me to focus on a few central passages to the frequent neglect of demonstrating textually their implications for the main themes. Besides, the gospel itself is not long and anything—even the suspicion of wrongheaded interpretation—that can motivate a firsthand reading will not have been entirely without purpose.

Flesh and spirit

The passage most frequently cited by scholars of gnostic Christianity again and again to show up the Gospel of Thomas's evaluation of the world of the senses runs:

Jesus said, "If the flesh came into being because of spirit, it is a wonder. But if spirit came into being because of the body, it is a wonder of wonders. Indeed, I am amazed at how this great wealth has made its home in this poverty." (29)

To read the phrase *wonder of wonders* as contrary-to-fact irony would require a grammatical form that the context does not provide, not to mention a dreadful wrench on the obvious meaning of the final phrase. Yet this is just what commentators have done, reading it to mean that spirit and flesh are opposed because of the necessary evil of spirit making a home for itself in flesh.[17]

If, however, we grant that the author, or team of authors, was a Christian believer appropriating gnostic insights to a Christian purpose and at the same time attempting to improve on it, there is little reason to force the passage into the mold of Gnosticism's worst doctrines about the body. Here we have Jesus, whom we have been led to believe through the first third of the text is a preacher of gnosis, expressing surprise at an idea that strays from received gnostic tradition: What if flesh and spirit come into being *because of each other*? That the weak and dying flesh is created to house the noble, undying spirit is wonder enough. But if it should happen that the spirit is created to enliven the flesh—that would be a wonder of wonders!

There seems to be no reason to read irony into this text. The only irony consists in still calling "poor" what has clearly been enriched, an irony that is enriched by the opposite meanings given to poverty in the text: as a sign of being a blessed elect (54) and as a metaphor for ignorance (3).

The preparation for this idea is already present in earlier sayings. The most important of these is the Christian idea of the "living Jesus" who is announced in the opening line of the gospel as having revealed himself to Thomas, whom tradition held to be the twin brother (Didymus) of Jesus. The implied symbolism of the true believer as an *alter Christus* (a title to be reserved for the priest in ages to come) is clear.[18] But this same Thomas who received the secret wisdom of Jesus (13) was the doubter whom the Gospel of John, the most gnostic of the canonical gospels and the only one to refer to him as the twin, has Jesus chide for not being satisfied with spiritual belief but demanding to feel the resurrected with his own hands. There is little chance that Thomas himself was the actual author of the gospel that bears his name, but this does not diminish the importance of his having been chosen as the symbolic recipient of its "secret" wisdom. If anything, it alerts us to bear the image of the doubting twin in mind.

A second, though more indirect, preparatory hint for a reversal of the gnostic stance appears almost immediately after the first:

> Jesus said, "Let him who seeks continue seeking until he finds. When he finds, he will be troubled. When he becomes troubled, he will be astonished, and he will rule over all. (2)

The familiar advice from the synoptic gospels, "Seek and you shall find," seems to imply that one will in fact find what one was seeking for. The Gospel of John, which does not include this saying, contains instead several references to Jesus rejecting what it is the disciples seek from him. In the passage just cited, the actual finding is said to cause trouble and then astonishment for the seeker. In the text, the point is directly applied to finding the kingdom of God in the last place one would think to look for it— within oneself—but the fact that it appears so early in the text (saying 3) seems to advise a much wider application.

Habits and their rehabilitation

A second passage frequently cited as belittling the bodily senses in fact shows clearly how the gospel shifts the focus away from the body to a more fundamental problem. This shift is important for a later restoration of awareness of the body. Jesus is asked by his disciples, "When will you become revealed to us and when shall we see you?" He answers:

> "When you disrobe without being ashamed and take up your garments and place them under your feet like little children and tread

on them, then [will you see] the son of the living one, and you will not be afraid." (37)

The image appears already in an earlier passage in which, replying to the question[19] what his disciples are like, Jesus says:

"They are like children who have settled in a field which is not theirs. When the owners of the field come, they will say, 'Let us have back our field.' They (will) undress in their presence in order to let them have back their field ...." (21)

Given the numerous allusions to clothing as a symbol of the flesh worn by the spirit, commentators have the image of taking off one's clothes and trampling on them as a command to disincarnate the spirit to prepare it for true knowledge.[20] Yet even within gnosticism there is no uniform symbolic meaning to clothing. For example, in the "Hymn of the Pearl" (Acts of Thomas) a young prince who is sent off to Egypt to recover a great treasure doffs the robes of his youth and disguises himself in the filthy garments of the foreign land. When he returns home, treasure in hand, he is presented with his old robe, which, when he puts it on, makes him whole. Before it had merely "fit the countours" of his person, now it covers his "entire self":

It seemed to me suddenly to become a mirror-image of myself: myself entire I saw in it and it entire I saw in myself, that we were two in separateness, and yet again one in the sameness of our forms.[21]

It is hard to see how there can be any question here of the mind simply casting the senses to one side.[22] On the contrary, the retrieval of the lost treasure reawakens one to the "robe" as an inseparable part of oneself. As the text puts it, the prince sees the robe "quiver all over with the movements of the gnosis."

Once the divesting is seen not as an end in itself but as a prelude to a revesting, the meaning of children standing in the field like original creations, "naked but not ashamed" (Gen 2.25), their clothes lying at their feet, changes dramatically. The clothes are no longer the pitiful casing of the spirit, but the necessary *habits* of perception that open the spirit to experience and knowledge. To conquer the shame of letting go of conventions is to take the first step towards the *rehabilitation* of perception. The immediately preceding advice of Jesus to his disciples not to be concerned about "what you will wear" (36) is not counsel to go around without wearing anything at all, but counsel not to worry about whether one's habits happen to conform to convention or not. As we shall see, the importance of distancing oneself from convention runs like an undercurrent throughout the Gospel of Thomas.

Seeing through worldly conventions

Even more than his counterpart in the canonical gospels, the Jesus of the Gospel of Thomas rejects reliance on ascetical and religious practices both because true reform lies not in outer conventions but in inner transformation (14), and because the kingdom of God belongs to the here and now (51). To realize this fact through recognizing oneself as the brother of the resurrected one is at the same time to realize it in the world.

On the one hand, inner transformation is said to be a power that radiates on its own. This is the sense of the saying that the one who has "found" will "rule over all" (2) and be able to move mountains by commanding them to move (106). On the other, it is a vocation to discipline in and responsibility for the world. This *double entendre* of "realizing the truth" is present in the idea that gnosis requires a re-cognition of the world. The link is the body:

> "Whoever has come to understand the world has found (only) a corpse, and whoever has found a corpse is superior to the world." (56)

> "He who has recognized the world has found the body, but he who has found the body is superior to the world." (80)

On the face of it, the two sayings appear to be identical in meaning, which is how commentators have taken it.[23] But this assumes that the "body" is after all no more than a "corpse," or in other words, that the only resurrection is a resurrection of the spirit. It seems preferable to respect the distinction that the text gives us. The decisive term here is *the world*.

For the gnostics, of course, the world is the creation of an evil demiurge, not an outpouring of a loving God. Provided one does not assume in advance that the Gospel of Thomas agrees with this view, the text naturally suggests that the "world" is no more than "worldly conventions."[24] In so doing, the passages just cited take opposite meanings. In the first, "recognizing the world" means seeing through conventional habits of thought as no more than a lifeless corpse; in the second, this recognition is said to recover a view of the body as something alive. In both cases, the limits of convention are lifted. The idea of "seeing through" conventions to "recover" the body is a clear instance of gnosis affirming the resurrected body, not denying it.

An earlier exchange between Jesus and the disciples confirms this reading. Hearing Jesus talk of the great struggle that is required to attain an inner kingdom the disciples ask Jesus to tell them "how our end will be." He scolds them for not even having started on the road and already anxious to know where it will end. Jesus goes on:

> "If you become my disciples and listen to my words, these stones will minister to you. For there are five trees in Paradise which remain undisturbed summer and winter and whose leaves do not fall. Whoever becomes acquainted with them will not experience death." (19)

The reference to the ministry of the stones echoes the earlier idea of "ruling over all" but the choice of stones is not incidental. A few sayings previous Thomas had just received three secret teachings from Jesus which he refuses to tell the others because they will pick up stones to throw at him and "a fire will come out of the stones and burn you up" (13).

That one to whom conventional truth has become transparent has superseded the charge of blasphemy is a frequent theme in Gnosticism, as in other esoteric literature. What is odd is the explanation given for why the stones obey the gnostic: the five trees in Paradise whose knowledge brings life beyond the reach of death.

The image of the life-giving trees in Paradise is, I believe, closely connected with the idea of "listening" to the words of Jesus, which is presented in the pericope above as something beyond mere discipleship. Indeed, the most oft-repeated phrase in the Gospel of Thomas is the injunction: "Whoever has ears to hear, let him hear." The "ears" Jesus is speaking of are not the ears of conventional perception that hear en masse, but the ear of the individual who is able to understand. Note the use of singular and plural forms in saying 33:

> "Preach from your (pl.) housetops that which you (sg.) will hear in your ear [in the other ear]."

The phrase at the end, which has been taken as an error in transcription[25] makes good sense understood as referring to the "inner ear" that listens to what others can only hear. The senses that truly perceive are truly alive, no longer deadened by the world of ordinary conventions. These are each, in the words of the Book of Revelation, like a "tree of life set in God's Paradise."[26]

Setting the senses beyond the mortifying influence of conventional modes of perception does not mean transcending the world but a being *in* the world but not *of* it, to use words familiar from the Gospel of John.[27] Hence Jesus advises his disciples to protect themselves from those who would invade their dwelling (21, 35, 103). The recovery, exercise, and safeguard of the senses from the deprivations of habit is an essential ingredient to insight, if not a measure of its truth:

> "I shall give you what no eye has seen and no ear heard and no hand has touched and what has never occurred to the human mind." (17)

What Jesus promises is no more noncorporeal than it is nonmental. It is a heightened experience of mind and body.

Becoming as little children

The paradigm of the liberated senses is, of course, Jesus himself. It is no coincidence that in contrasting himself with the "world," he uses the language of the senses:

> "I took my place in the midst of the world, and I appeared to them in flesh. I found all of them intoxicated; I found none of them thirsty." (28)

The sense-deprivations that I have referred to as forms of mass asceticism are not in the first place a function of appetite but of gluttony. Here, too, the reason Jesus' appearance goes unnoticed is that the senses of his listeners have been intoxicated to the point of stupefaction. The revival of the senses is also a revival of the appetite for substantial, enlivening satisfactions. Alienation from appetite is the result of addiction to their noncollaborative, passive satisfaction. We have to learn, in the words of the Gospel of Thomas, to become "thirsty" again.

The most common image in the text for the purification of appetite is that of becoming as little children who "know the place of life" (4). The aim is not of course a return to juvenile ignorance (the children in saying 21, for instance, have made themselves a home in someone else's field, and in the following saying are no more than suckling infants), but the ability to experience the deepest desires of body and mind simply, as if for the first time.

Only those with this childlike quality as "the elect of the living father" (50) can be "acquainted with the kingdom" (46). The election of these "children of the light" (a term also found in John 12.36) does not imply initiation into a body of arcane doctrines. The secret teachings of the Gospel of Thomas are very much an open secret. The elite who understand it are not the hand-picked disciples of elder adepts, but those who have the courage to strip themselves down to their native childlikeness and discover the truth within themselves.[28]

If becoming like Jesus means becoming like a little child, the implication is that Jesus is himself like a little child. The Gospel of

Thomas does not in fact draw this conclusion, but it does provide an additional reason for the popularity of the Infancy Gospel of Thomas, a collection of folktales compiled about the same time and in the same gnostic atmosphere. Be that as it may, the child-like following of the heart's desire is the very thing that the Jesus of the Gospel of Thomas reproaches the scribes and pharisees for having repressed. "They have taken the keys of knowledge," he says, "and hidden them. They themselves have not entered, nor have they allowed to enter those who wish to" (39). A later saying that likens them to dogs in the manger that neither eat nor allow the oxen to eat (102) suggests further a wrongful curbing of appetites.[29]

Defeminizing salvation

The positive allusions to appetites of body and mind immediately raise the question of the attitude towards gender and sexual activity. Virtually all commentators are agreed that "the Gospel of Thomas advances a strict sexual ascesis."[30] Aside from passages cited earlier, which do not support such a view on their own, the sayings that deal with women have seemed to provide the conclusive evidence. I am not convinced.

As in John 4, it is the disciples who are surprised to find Jesus conversing with women, the disciples who in the Gospel of Thomas are painted as a particularly dull-witted lot (Thomas being the exception, as we noted earlier) and whose questions almost always miss the mark of what Jesus has said. It is safe to presume that their views are the very conventions that Jesus is seeking to overturn.

The gospel ends with this exchange:

Simon Peter said to them, "Let Mary leave us, for women are not worthy of life."

Jesus said, "I myself shall lead her in order to make her male, so that she too may become a living spirit resembling you males. For every women who will make herself male will enter the kingdom of heaven." (114)

The idea of defeminizing as a condition for salvation is an undeniable part of the gnostic tradition. If Jesus' words are taken out of context—or, which amounts to the same thing, if the saying is treated as simply one more pearl strung on the general thread of gnostic thought—this passage can only ring harsh on the modern ear. Such a judgment is unfair to the Gospel of Thomas.

In context, the comment of Peter is a crude misunderstanding of Jesus' final recapitulation of his teachings about seeing and transcending the world's conventions in general, and the conventions about flesh and spirit in particular:

"Whoever finds the world and becomes rich, let him renounce the world." (110).

"Whoever finds himself is superior to the world." (111)

"Woe to the flesh that depends on the soul; woe to the soul that depends on the flesh." (112)

"The kingdom of the father is spread out upon the earth, and men do not see it." (113)

As is often the case in the Gospel of Thomas, the disciple bases his question on bias and word-association: Does not the specification of one who finds *himself* and the *men* justify the dismissal of women? Jesus answers the question by disowning its ignorance.

The woman that Jesus would *lead* is the same woman that Peter would *leave* behind. And while Jesus sees resemblances between the sexes in spirit that challenge the discriminations of worldly convention, Peter can only see the differences of the flesh. On the assumption that earlier references in the gospel to the flesh had all been derogatory, it is possible to argue that the kingdom of God is for disembodied spirits, where there is no male or female.[31] And from this one can go the step further and argue that woman is the gnostic symbol for the corrupted realm of matter in general.[32] Yet these are the very assumptions that the first phrase of saying 112—"Woe to the flesh that depends on the soul"—discards.[33] For the Gospel of Thomas, only an interdependence of opposites will do.

What the Gospel of Thomas *does* seem to have taken from the gnostic cosmology is the much older image of an originally androgynous human, temporarily separated into male and female but inwardly longing for reunion.[34] Here it is applied merely to the realm of spiritual insight, the kingdom, where this reunion can take place.[35] By accepting the woman into the ranks of the "led," Jesus implies that it is equally important for the male to make himself female in order to enter the kingdom.

The idea of an equality in discipleship is also present in an earlier exchange in the gospel between Jesus and the mysterious figure of Salome:

> Jesus said, "Two will rest on a bed: the one will die and the other will live."
>
> Salome said, "Who are you, man, that you have come up on my couch and eaten from my table?"
>
> Jesus said to her, "I am he who exists from the undivided. I was given some of the things of my father."
>
> [Salome said,] "I am your disciple."
>
> [Jesus said to her,] "Therefore I say, if he[36] is destroyed he will be filled with light, but if he is divided, he will be filled with darkness." (61)

The "one" who dies here is the one who is cut off from the "other." The individual who first breaks away to "stand alone" from conventional relationships (4, 16) is fulfilled only when the reality of the other is restored. I conclude that the import of the passage that "the one will die and the other will live" is that dividedness ends in darkness and ignorance, while the destruction of dividedness leads to light and understanding. But the imagery of achieving wholeness at bed and table also links the most basic appetites of the flesh to the world of the spirit. For it is as a "man" that Salome addresses him. Jesus identifies himself as "from the undivided" and Salome (whose name signifies a "harmony" of

opposites[37]) as his "disciple." The overcoming of dividedness on
the bed turns the "one" into an "other" who lives. As a later saying
notes, it is only when the bridegroom leaves the bridal chamber
that the two must fast and pray (104). As long as they are one,
there is no distinction between the appetites of the spirit and
those of the body. This image of the resurrected, though still lan-
guishing under the weight of body-soul distinctions, has extracted
itself here from the gnostic depreciation of the senses and the
feminine.

There is far more in the Gospel of Thomas than I have been able
to touch on in these few pages, and no doubt the passages cited
above will reflect rather different concerns to other readers. Such
is the fate of a text cloaked in the ambivalence of the gnostic
movement and its Christian connections.

　　Much the same mystery wraps itself about the scientific-
technological myth of our own times. For all its appeal and obvious achievement, there is a barbarous, despotic side to our myth
that demands of religion both a critical distance and a critical
response. I have tried to suggest that the deprivation of the senses
belongs to this dark side of our modern myth; and that the Gospel
of Thomas, many of whose ideas have long clung to the underbelly of the Christian tradition, is very much *our evangel*. In the
same way that the pagan, rural religions of Europe and the Americas long kept alive a sense of nature that had been absent from
Christian theology, perhaps there is still more to be learned from
civilizations less overwhelmed by the allurements of development
than we about freeing ourselves from the asceticisms of our age
and restoring to religions like Buddhism and Christianity their
care for the senses.

NOTES

[1] The version I am using here appears in the ninth-century *Fan i ming i chi*
翻譯名義集 (T. 54.1140c), which quotes it as coming from the *Ta fang teng ta chi*

ching 大方等大集經 (T. 13), a massive translation of the *Mahāsaṃnipāta Sūtra* compiled in the latter part of the sixth century. (An extensive search of the supposed source did not turn up the story, however.) The text is interpolated with a commentary attributed to the T'ien-t'ai tradition.

Another version appears in the older *Pin t'ou lu t'u lo she wei yu t'o yen wang shuo fa ching* 賓頭盧突羅闍爲優陀延王説法經 (T. 32.787a), where it ends pessimistically, as the bees swarm out of the hive, from which the honey had dripped, to attack the man. However, the version I have cited appears with a similar commentary and ending in another sixth-century text, a San-lun commentary on the *Vimalakīrtinirdeśa-sutra* by Chi-ts'ang 吉藏 (維摩 經義疏, T. 38.934c). Of particular note is the fact that the passage being commented on is the hymn on the body, in which the sick and failing Vimalakīrti teaches that the body with all its gusts is ultimately disgusting, and counsels his listeners to turn their attention to the spiritual body of the Buddha. In the course of his remarks, the body is referred to as an "old well," whence the connection with the parable.

Lamotte notes a similar use of this parable by Kumārajīva in a late fourth-century commentary attributed to one of his disciples on the same passage (T. 1775.342b). Étienne Lamotte, *The Teaching of Vimalakīrti*, trans. by S. Boin (London: Pali Text Society, 1976), 37, note d. As in Chi-tsang's version, the drops of honey allay the fugitive's fears by satisfying his senses, which suggests the authenticity of the version.

A well-known English version of the tale, falsely identified as coming from the thirteenth-century Japanese collection known as the *Shasekishū* 沙石集, has the man chased by a tiger, clinging to a vine over the edge of a precipice, and eating a wild strawberry. I have been unable to locate this version anywhere, but the tale is an old one, probably pre-Buddhist, and it is not impossible that such a version exists. See Paul Reps, *Zen Flesh, Zen Bones* (Garden City, N. Y.: Doubleday, n.d.), 122.

In *My Confession* Tolstoy cites substantially the same version of the tale I have used here in recounting his bouts with a despair that neither the wisdom of East nor West could conquer. William James recalls the passage to show the depths of the despair to which Tolstoy had sunk, but also later notes that it was precisely in savoring the ordinary pleasures of life that he was to find release from despair: "Tolstoy was one of those primitive oaks of men to whom the superfluities and insincerities, the cupidities, complications, and cruelties of our polite civilization are profoundly unsatisfying, and for whom *the eternal veracities lie with more natural and animal things....* And though not many of us can imitate Tolstoy, not having enough, perhaps, of the aboriginal human marrow in our bones, most of us may at least feel as if it might be better for us if we could." *The Varieties of Religious Experience* (New York: Modern Library, 1902), 151, 183, emphasis added.

² Although the images are too old for these interpretations to be uniform either in Buddhism or in its pre-Buddhist sources, the image of being caught in an old

well does appear elsewhere as an allegory of the emprisonment of the senses. For example, the *Ta ch'eng p'u sa ts'ang cheng fa ching* 大乘菩薩藏正法經 (T. 11.840b–c) uses this image and likens the pursuit of old age, sickness, death, and suffering to two mice and four snakes.

[3] *Jākata*, book 4, no. 334. The Buddha identifies himself as the ascetic and Ānanda as the king.

[4] E. H. Johnson, *The Buddhacarita or Acts of the Buddha* (Delhi: Motilal Banarsidass, 1972), 473–8. Edward Conze, *Buddhist Scriptures* (Hardmondsworth: Penguin, 1959), 47–51. The Chinese translation, *Fo so hsing tsan* 佛所 行讚 (T. 4) has simplified many of these images or omitted them.

[5] *Samyutta-Nikāya*, 12.11.

[6] This same tendency to take *sight* as representative of all the senses and then generalize about their salvation through *insight* is rather common in Buddhist sources. In the sūtra sighted in note 2 above, for example, the senses are referred to cumulatively as "sight etc." and are said to be mere appearance or dream-like imagery. From this it is a short step to say that the whole body is without substance, just as a banana plant is a tree without a trunk (T.11 840a–b). This influence of the metaphor on the theory is significant here, in that the unreflected tendency to identify sense deprivation with the blindness of *avidyā* may lend religious support to the mass anesthesia of modern media and transportation. Attention to this question would suggest complementing the familiar "Buddha eye" with a Buddha nose, a Buddha ear (which in fact appears in the *Abhidharmakośa*), and so on. See notes 25–26 and accompanying text below.

[7] Sermon 40 (Pfeiffer), cited in the translation of Maurice O'Connell Walshe, *Meister Eckhart: Sermons and Treatises* (Longmead, England: Watkins, 1987), vol. 1, 283.

[8] Gottfried von Strassburg, *Tristan* (Wiesbaden: F. A. Brockhaus, 1978), 15, lines 230–40.

[9] See *Hadewijch: The Complete Works*, ed. by Mother Columba Hart (New York: Paulist, 1980), 280–2. Paul Mommaers, who first drew my attention to these passages, has written a helpful essay, "Hadewijch: A Feminist in Conflict," *Louvain Studies* 13 (1988): 58–81.

[10] In addition to translations included in other works cited in the following notes, I have kept before me the authoritative version of the Coptic Gnostic Library, vol. 20, *Nag Hammadi Codex* II, 2-7, ed. by Bentley Layson (Leiden: Brill, 1989). The enumeration here follows the Coptic text.

[11] See Elaine Pagels, *The Gnostic Gospels* (New York: Random House, 1989), ch. 7 and page 144. R. Winterhalter's *The Fifth Gospel* (New York: Harper and Row, 1988) is far more adventurous in discovering a whole range of modern notions like

that of the "true Self" in the text. In contrast, Michael Fieger's *Das Thomasevangelium* (Münster: Aschendorff, 1991), a lengthy study of the Coptic text, avoids the lapse into modern psychology entirely, following the example of the earlier commentary of Robert Grant and David Freedman's *The Secret Sayings of Jesus* (London: Collins, 1960). In fact, the decisive passage appears here—as in many other cases—to have been simply copied from Grant and Freedman (28), including the outdated understanding of the Delphic oracle's "know thyself."

[12] Hans Jonas, *The Gnostic Religion* (Boston: Beacon, 1963), 123–4. For Plato and Augustine, see the full textual argument of Charles Taylor in *Sources of the Self* (Cambridge, Mass.: Harvard University Press, 1989), ch. 6 and 7. In the case of the *Gospel of Thomas*, it should be noted that the Coptic version is a translation, probably mid-fourth century, of the original Greek, of which only fragments remain, certainly not enough to suggest a clear distinction between key terms dealing with body and mind.

[13] A detailed exposition of the wide variety of explanations regarding the mutual influence of gnosticism and Christianity and the relative merits of each can be found in Hugh Montefiore and H. E. W. Turner, *Thomas and the Evangelists* (Naperville, Ill.: Alec Allenson, 1962). For a briefer and more up to date account, see Edwin Yamauchi, *Pre-Christian Gnosticism* (London: Tyndale, 1973), 89–91.

[14] Cited in Montefiore and Turner, *Thomas and the Evangelists*, 84.

[15] See Helmut Koester's "Introduction" to the work in *Nag Hammadi Codex*, 38; Montefiore and Turner, *Thomas and the Evangelists*, 21–2.

[16] There seems to be no indication of mnemonic linking, and there is much debate about just what the main themes of the work are. These are matters, however, that require a bigger talent than I am able to bring to the text.

[17] See, for example, Pagels, *The Gnostic Gospels*, 26; Grant and Freedman, *The Secret Sayings of Jesus*, 148; Fieger, *Das Thomasevangelium*, 115. Jacques-É. Ménard, *L'Évangile selon Thomas* (Leiden: Brill, 1975), 124. Of all the commentaries I have seen, only a sampling of which has been included in these notes, Fieger's adheres most rigidly to his expectations about the gnostic devaluation of the body, the cumulative effect of which is to to divert the flow of his commentary further and further away from the text.

[18] Translated literally, the triple name of the author—Didymos (Greek) Judas (Hebrew) Thomas (Aramaic) means "The Twin, Praise God!, The Twin." The middle name, Judas, functions like a copulative to unite the conventional and the gnostic meanings of being a brother of Jesus. Ménard argues that is is a real proper name (*L'Évangile selon Thomas*, 76). W. C. van Unnik, *Newly Discovered Gnostic Writings* (Naperville, Ill.: Alec Allenson, 1960), conjectures that the repetition of

the term Didymus after the Aramaic name Thomas indicates that the author "did not know about the linguistic connection and took both terms to be personal names" (49). I find this an odd argument.

[19] The questioner is called Mary, variously identified by commentators as Mary Magdalene or Mariham, whom the Naassene sect believed received a secret tradition through James the Righteous. Saying 12 has Jesus recommend James as the one the disciples are to follow after he is gone.

[20] Grant and Freedman mention passages in the fathers identifying this image of stripping down as coming from the Naassenes and from the Gospel of the Egyptians. *The Secret Sayings of Jesus*, 153. Montefiore and Turner see the trampling as "a contempt for and annulment of sex." *Thomas and the Evangelists*, 30. See also Ménard, *L'Évangile selon Thomas* 137.

[21] Cited after Jonas, *The Gnostic Religion*, 115. Jonas refers the youthful robe to the Mandean idea of the "earthly casing" in which the spirit languishes (113, n.4 and 56) while the later robe is a "the celestial form of the invisible because temporarily obscured self" (124). On the robe as an *alter ego*, see 122–3. For a clear example of this use in the Nag Hammadi texts, see the *Treatise on Resurrection*, where the donning of the robe is said to indicate a resurrection of the spirit that "swallows" resurrection of the soul and the flesh(45:28).

[22] For the argument that the changing of clothes "has to do with the search for a more effective disembodiment," see Otto Betz and Tim Schramm, *Perlenlied und Thomas Evangelium* (Zurich: Benzinger, 1985), 48–9.

[23] Fieger, *Das Thomasevangelium*, 222; Grant and Freedman, *The Secret Sayings of Jesus*, 164, 179. Ménard attributes the difference in the two passages to a simple error of translation (*L'Évangile selon Thomas*, 158).

[24] In saying 11, Jesus tells his disciples: "This heaven will pass away, and the one above it will pass away," which seems clearly to run counter to the gnostic belief that the heaven above this one—the realm of the true God—will one day conquer the multi-tiered heavens of the demiurge's creation.

[25] *Nag Hammadi Codex*, 67n. Ménard disagrees (*L'Évangile selon Thomas*, 24). Note the similar importance of the singular tense in saying 5.

[26] "If anyone has ears to hear, let him listen to what the Spirit is saying to the churches: those who prove victorious I will feed from the tree of life set in God's paradise" (2.7). The idea that the savant will "not experience death" appears already in the first saying of the Gospel of Thomas.

[27] I resist here the idea of the trees in paradise as representing a recovery of the sensual in the mere realm of imagination. The idea, while not unfamiliar to gnostic thought, is not restricted to it as we see, for example, in the *Shepherd of Hermas*, a work read as scripture in second-century Christian communities and considered as

such by Irenaeus. The text ends with a vision in which the Angel of Repentance rewards one who repented of a sin of sexual fantasy with the company of twelve virgins who pass the night in sport with the former sinner, dancing, kissing, and embracing him—"as helpers, that thou mayest be the better able to keep the commandments." Cited from J. B. Lightfoot, M. R. James, H. B. Swete, *Excluded Books of the New Testament* (London: Eveleigh Nash and Grayson, 1927), 9.11 (374), 10.3 (401).

[28] The distinguishing mark of the "father's presence" in these children of the light is said to be "movement and repose." Elsewhere, Jesus tells his listeners that in order to stay alive and not be consumed by the world, they should "look for a place for yourself within repose" (60). Although the text offers no other hint to the meaning of this cryptic phrase, it is not uncommon in esoteric traditions East and West to indicate action that comes from an inner harmony.

The Gospel of Thomas speaks of the awakened one as "the solitary" (49, in Greek, *monakos*). See also note 24.

[29] As Winterhalter points out, the image of the dog in the manger is to be found in one of Aesop's tales (*The Fifth Gospel*, 107).

[30] Betz and Schramm, *Perlenlied und Thomas Evangelium*, 98; Fieger, *Das Thomasevangelium*, 131.

[31] Grant and Freedman end their book on the sentence: "The high point of Thomas's eschatology is thus reached, at the end of his gospel, with the obliteration of sex." *The Secret Sayings of Jesus*, 198.

[32] Fieger, *Das Thomasevangelium*, 286.

[33] Jesus' allusion to the father (and by implication, himself) as "not born of woman" (15) does not in any way argue for the influence of the gnostic attitude is unfounded. The phrase is simply an idiom for "all creatures of God" (see Job 14.1). Otherwise, there would be no explaining how saying 46 can mention Adam as "among those born of women."

[34] See Ménard, *L'Évangile selon Thomas*, 210.

[35] I think it not without significance that Jesus uses men and women for similar allegories of the kingdom: like a man who had a treasure hidden in his field without knowing it (109) and like a woman who took a little leaven and concealed it in some dough (96).

[36] Grant and Freedman translated the particle as *it* and suggest that it refers to the bed, in which case it confirms the Naassene rejection of sexual intercourse (*The Secret Sayings of Jesus*, 167–8).

[37] The figure of Salome appears frequently in the Nag Hammadi texts and elsewhere (for example, the Gospel of the Egyptians, the Birth of Mary, and the Apoc-

alypse of James), without any apparent consistency of symbolic meaning. For further details, see Ménard, *L'Évangile selon Thomas*, 162. There is no reason here to assume that in this passage she is any more or less a symbol of the feminine than Jesus is of the masculine.

Converting Buddhism to Christianity, Christianity to Buddhism

The essay was originally solicited for a collection on interreligious dialogue published by Risshō Kōseikai's Central Institute for Academic Research. I chose the topic for the simple reason that "mutual conversion" had begun to turn up in things I was writing like a kind of self-evident cliché and was ricochetting back to me from different directions. I felt it was time I gave some thought to the matter.

As nearly as I can figure, I picked the term up from John Cobb. For as long as I have lived and worked in Asia, I have believed him to be the soul of dialogue, and I am sure this is not the only idea of his that I absorbed on that belief.

In this essay, I have tried to take up the commonly heard criticism that interreligious dialogue involves a suspension of faith, or at least a suspension of the desire to propagate the faith, and that its aim is to articulate a syncretistic, culturally transcendent form of religion tailored to the demands of interreligious scholarship.

I disagree with both conclusions. At the same time, there is every indication that the mutual transformation of Buddhism and Christianity has only just begun, and that that transformation will outlast efforts to derail the process into the immediate satisfaction of a simple faceoff between traditions or a simple fusion of the two.

Originally published as「仏教とキリスト教の相互的回心」
『宗教間対話運動の課題』[Issues in interreligious dialogue],中央学術研究所 (Tokyo: 1997), 16–25. The English version was published in *Japanese Religions* 22 (1997): 107–17.

THE AGE OF RELIGIOUS conquest is over. Hopes of winning the whole world over to a single religious organization still linger from the past, but they ring shallow and out of key with the religious consciousness that has taken shape in the twentieth century and is propelling us into the next millennium. The interreligious dialogue that has come to flower over the past twenty years among world religions—a flowering in which Buddhism and Christianity have taken the lead—has been instrumental in redirecting religious faith away from the dream of redrawing the religious geography of the world, and towards the dream of cultivating insights and virtues suited to coexistence in a religiously plural world.

While it has been the classical world religions have taken the lead in the dialogue, the outcome is that the very idea of a "world religion" now needs to be redefined, and that redefinition woven into the religious expression and ritual habits of ordinary believers. Proportions of membership, institutional wealth, cultural influence, doctrinal development, and international expansion, all standards suited to measure the progress of organized religion in the past, are no longer normative for a religiously plural world. The world religion of the future will be judged by a different standard, a standard new to human history and as yet only dimly perceived.

Interreligious dialogue is only one of the factors that have contributed to this change in climate. The dialogue is neither the primary impulse towards nor is it a model for the great transformation that I believe lies in store for historical and popular religion. Dialogue has helped to disarm organized religion of

weapons of mass conversion and at the same time has helped preserve the intellectual credibility of doctrinal tradition, but its
atmosphere is too rarefied to produce a general spirituality. It can
open windows in the citadel of self-understanding that established religions have built for themselves; the fresh air must come
from the outside. By the same token, to close the interreligious
dialogue off from ordinary believers as a field for specialists is to
forget that it blew into our age in a much wider whirlwind of religious sentiment. If dialogue needs to be done from within established religion, it must always be done with one's head out the
window.

That said, I do not see any way for traditional world religions
like Buddhism and Christianity to produce a general spirituality
for their faithful in a religiously plural world except they first
accept as their rightful inheritance the entire religious wealth of
humanity. This acceptance calls for a major conversion. It is no
coincidence that widespread disenchantment with organized religion in our times goes hand in hand with an increase in religiosity. Religious establishments have fallen too far out of touch with
the religious sentiment of the day for even a complete reuphol-
stering of terminology or a radical overhaul of the bureaucracy to
restore. Part of getting back in touch with the religious spirit of
our age, perhaps the greatest part, has to do with a change of heart
towards the truth of other religions. By this I mean not only coex-
isting amicably in the religious story of our times, but also participating mutually in the spread and the deepening of one another's
truth.

THE MISSION IMPERATIVE

Among the complaints that come most frequently to those
engaged actively in interreligious dialogue, even at the abstract
levels, is that such work promotes a kind of à la carte religiosity
that leaves the content of faith to the discretion of individual
believers and undermines tradition. Dialogue is said to begin
from an epistemological commitment to the relativity of truth,

which it then shellacs with a shiny coat of "open-mindedness" and "tolerance" designed to appeal to modern sensitivities. The result is that those working away at the dialogue in academia land themselves in one or the other form of theoretical syncretism, while those trying to find a place for faith in their workaday lives are left with a do-it-yourself tradition. Beliefs, rituals, scriptures, language, architecture, art, music, costume—all are tossed into a single potpourri of "religion" and blended to the lowest common denominator.

This is not the place to take up the question of the meaning of "absolute truth." Nor is there time to untangle the prejudices surrounding the term "syncretism." More important is that the sentiment behind the complaint be addressed, namely, that without a clear identity that sets one's religious tradition off from others, there is no way to spread the truth of one's belief or affiliate new members. The sentiment is hardly misguided. Obviously, the more religious contents are left to individual choice, the less chance an established institution has of preserving its past and growing in the future. Without the two wings of self-preservation and self-diffusion, religious tradition cannot get off the ground. As the two world religions that have gone furthest in the interreligious dialogue, Buddhism and Christianity cannot simply ignore these fears of what is to become of their mission towards one another and towards the masses of humanity in a religiously plural world.

To begin with, it is clear that both Christianity and Buddhism are *fundamentally missionary* in orientation. For Christians, the scriptural source is clear and well-known to all believers. In three of the four gospels Jesus concludes his final instruction to his disciples with the "Great Commission" to "go forth and make disciples of all nations."[1] While the gospel of Matthew adds the note that they are to "baptize" them, this seems to be an addition reflecting liturgical practice of the later community, since Jesus did not in fact baptize his disciples. In any case, the passage does not as such enjoin Christian believers to form an institution and then affiliate as many members to it as possible, but simply to spread the teachings of Jesus as "Good News for all creation."

Despite its prominent place at the conclusion of the gospels, the Great Commission was not always at the center of Christian consciousness. Indeed, the waves of Protestant and then Catholic missionary bands that swelled in the early years of the nineteenth century were an attempt to shake Western churches out of their parochialism and remind them of the fields to be harvested for Christ in Africa and Asia. A century later the World Missionary Conference, held in Edinburgh in 1910, met in an atmosphere of anticipation of the collapse of non-Christian religions in the twentieth century: "The spectacle of the advance of the Christian Church along many lines of action to the conquest of the five great religions of the modern world is one of singular interest and grandeur."[2]

Obviously the "Christian Century" turned out differently than expected. By the time of the second missionary conference at Jerusalem in 1928, the black tide of secular paganism had replaced the other world religions as the principal enemy to be conquered. At the third meeting, held in India in 1938, Karl Barth's famous dialectic between the plurality of religious form and the single word of God revealed in Christ was very much to the fore in attempts to blunt the aggressive edge of the mission to other religions in favor of more temperate means of calling people out from the darkness of their religions into the light of the Christian revelation. After the Second World War Catholic theologians began to suggest that there was salvation in other religions, or at least a kind of "anonymous Christianity," and that competitive missions should yield to the common search for truth. This thinking was to bear fruit both in the proclamation of the Second Vatican Council (1965) and three years later at the General Assembly of the World Council of Churches at Uppsala.

Today Christians find themselves at the end of the movement that began in the nineteenth century, but the words of the Great Commission continue to echo in the background of all their talk of interreligious dialogue. Indeed the Christian missionary orientation may even be stronger and purer at the end of the twentieth century than it was in at its triumphalistic beginning. Thanks to the dialogue with Buddhism, it is certainly different.

The nature and composition of the Buddhist scriptures all but preclude the idea of a universally accepted *locus classicus* for Buddhism's missionary orientation. Still, there is no doubt that the Buddha enjoined that the Dharma be promoted abroad, beyond the frontiers of its origins. In the *Mahāvagga* we find just such an injunction delivered to the first monastic community in the formula:

> Go ye now, my brother monks, and wander for the gain and welfare of the many, out of compassion for the world.... And let not two of you go the same way.

In the next chapter we find the monks returning with persons from faraway regions and foreign lands, asking that the Buddha confer ordination on them. Seeing how the travel had exhausted them, the Buddha does not withdraw or scale down his injunction to spread the Dharma abroad, but extends the power of ordination to the wandering missionaries so that they do not have constantly to be returning home:

> Confer in the different regions and different countries the ordinations yourself on those who desire to receive them.[3]

The aim of the Buddha was to convert the whole world, from the gods in heaven to people at the farthest reaches of earth. Leaving the world (*pabbjā, shukke*) was required of all his followers, but the monastic order was given the further mandate of going forth to spread the Dharma. A century later King Asoka would carry the missionary zeal of the Buddha further in the form of *Dharma-vijaya*, a systematic policy of moral persuasion whose aim was love, whose compass was "all living creatures," and whose insurance was a centralized government with officials stationed in key places throughout the empire.[4] The story of Buddhism's expansion throughout Asia is tribute both to the missionary enthusiasms of the founder and the influence of Asoka's monumental evangelical ambitions.

Never having developed a missiological theory and lacking in ecumenical organization, however, modern Buddhism was not equipped to launch a united missionary front to the West comparable to the regiments of Christian missionaries carrying the gospel to traditional Buddhist lands. In the 1930s T'ai-hsu and leaders of the Chinese Buddhist Association made an attempt to gather support from Buddhists in other Asian lands to undertake a world-wide propagation of the Dharma and a "uniting of all existing forms of civilization."[5] Similar efforts were made by the Mahabodhi Society in India, which collaborated initially with the Theosophical Society to set up a mission in English in 1925, but again nothing on the scale of the Christian missions.

Since the Second World War the advance of ecumenical cooperation among Buddhists of different countries and the rise of lay Buddhist sects have brought with them hopes of the Buddha Dharma as an antidote to the general spiritual malaise of modern civilization. Missionary movements from several Buddhist lands have made considerable gains in membership and institutional strength in the traditional Judaeo-Christian lands of Europe and the Americas—enough to prompt in response counter-efforts at "re-evangelization" in both Protestant and Catholic Christianity. At the same time, Buddhist groups and individuals that have accepted the invitation of Christianity to engage in dialogue have stimulated Christians to a serious rethinking of theology and given Buddhism a new forum for reflecting on the meaning of the Buddha's teachings and their transmission today.

The Buddhist-Christian encounter has brought together these two great missionary religions in human history to discuss common concerns in an interreligious world. The idea that either of them should forsake their missionary orientation or weaken its zeal simply in order to enhance the dialogue is self-defeating. For each to be true to what it is, the dialogue must always be a forum of conversion. The question is what *kind* of conversion.

THE VERNACULAR IMPERATIVE

Throughout their respective histories, both Christianity and Buddhism have experimented with "accommodation" and "confrontation" in their contact with other cultures and religions. Both have known how to use the weapons of steel and weapons of culture to spread themselves institutionally, and both have produced their share of intellectual giants who have known how to harmonize their sacred teachings amicably with other ways of belief and thought. In either case, the goal of the strategy was the same: to win converts over to one's own way of belief.

For many, interreligious dialogue is simply a continuation of the one strategy or the other: either it provides a free forum for answering doubts and clearing up misunderstandings about beliefs or it sets up a formal debate in which conflicting beliefs can compete intellectually with one another. This is to miss the point. The genius of interreligious dialogue belongs to neither accommodation nor confrontation, and the reason is that the conversion it aims at is not a shift of affiliation or a decision for one tradition and against another. Conceptually speaking, the dialogue aims neither at replacing some beliefs with others nor at merely harmonizing them, but at translating the self-understanding of one tradition into that of another.

Not that this is a particularly novel idea. Just as missionary orientation is fundamental to Buddhism and Christianity, so is the *vernacular orientation* needed to loosen the hold that one particular time or culture or way of thinking has on teachings held sacred in order that they might enter other times and circumstances freely.

For the early Christian community, the link between the orientation to mission and the orientation to the vernacular is symbolized in the event of Pentecost.[6] The core disciples of Jesus, all of them Galileans, were gathered together in a room in Jerusalem when a "powerful wind" came upon them and they began to preach in strange tongues. Jerusalem was a cosmopolitan city with people from nations near and far speaking a variety of languages.

The commotion attracted crowds of people who were astonished. "How does it happen that each of us hears them in his own native language?" Some laughed it off as the effects of the new vintage of wine, but Peter, the leader of the disciples, stood up and assured them that they were inspired with the Holy Spirit to talk of what Jesus had taught them and that this same Spirit would be given to all who accept Jesus and repented. On this day the first converts to Christianity were made.

The "gift of tongues," which seems to have been common in the early Christian community, was a simple marvel restricted to those who witnessed it. The real miracle of Pentecost was that the teachings of Jesus, which had grown out of a particular religious heritage and cultural environment, translated intelligibly into the languages of "people from every nation under heaven." The cultural divisions that were symbolized in the tale of the tower of Babel had been transcended by the simple message of a carpenter from Galilee.

The best comparable symbolic event I know of is a story that appears in the Pali canon. Two monks, brahmans by birth, approached the Buddha with the complaint: "Lord, monks of various clans and races are corrupting your words be repeating them in their own dialects. Let us record your teachings in Vedic." But the Buddha would have none of it. "How can you be so deluded? This will not lead the unconverted to convert but will only drive the converted away." Instead, he summoned all the monks together and instructed them that his words were *not* to be set down in Vedic. "Who does so would commit a sin. I authorize you, monks, to learn the Buddha's words each in his own dialect."[7] This same position is attested to and elaborated on in Chinese versions of the same incident.[8]

From the start, the missions of Christianity and Buddhism were to preach a *universal* truth, not a *uniform* one. As the gnostics would say, its truth was to be like a circle whose center is everywhere and whose circumference nowhere. The Pentecostal tongues and the Buddha's condemnation of sacred language both point to a common and fundamental conversion of tradition to vernacular culture. It is this conversion, not the affiliation of new membership or the conquest of cultural authority, that is the model for interreligious conversion.

MUTUAL CONVERSION

The idea of mutual conversion, of participating in the spread and deepening of one another's truth, did not occur to Buddha or Jesus, nor is it found in the sacred texts of either tradition. It is a new aim for which the flowering of the Buddhist-Christian dialogue is both the index and the stimulus. It is not the metanoia of the individual who turns away from one set of values to embrace another. It does not ask for a shift of one's basic frame of symbolic reference. Neither is it the same as catechesis or initiation into a particular sect. It is a meeting of traditions—or, which is to say the same thing, of individuals raised within doctrinally different traditions—on a common ground of religiosity that belongs to neither but is claimed rightly by both. That common ground does not need the approval of any scripture and gains nothing by theological justification. It is part of our birthright as persons living in our age. It is, we might say, part of the mystery of what is "in the air": for the most part invisible, breathed in and out unconsciously, but always there to inspire the dialogue, always waiting patiently for the dialogue to transform into a music that faith can understand.

To avoid confusion, it is best to distinguish interreligious dialogue from *interreligious encounter*. This latter is broader, including everything from joint social action to cultivation of one another's techniques of prayer and meditation to sharing in religious rituals. Dialogue is something different. As the Greek root of *dialogue* suggests, it means gleaning ideas and paraphrasing them in different dialects; it means arguing, discussing, criticizing, and making up one's mind in words read and heard, spoken and written. As such, it has no aim outside of itself. As Jan Van Bragt says, its aim is to be "aimless," a "holy adventure" that secondary agenda betray.[9] To put the dialogue at the service of proselytizing is to squander its strengths; to turn it into a field of expertise, to open departments or graduate programs in its name, or to fit it out with rules is to weaken its scandalum. Its only agenda is the conversion of participants on the field of dialogue to a new way of seeing. What is done with what has been seen must take place outside of the forum of dialogue itself. If one enters the dialogue with an outside agenda, the conversion is blinded from the start; if everything that is done is done in the dialogue, the conversion is empty in the end.

The conversion of seeing in dialogue is, in the first place, a "turning towards the other." Unless Buddhism keeps Christianity as its "other" and vice-versa, there is nothing to turn towards. Cafeteria-style eclecticism may be—and in any case in fact *is*—a viable spiritual choice for many today. Harmonizing differences and accenting similarities, however magnanimous the gesture in compensating for former enmities, is unacceptable in the context of the dialogue insofar as it serves to erase or debilitate the sense of otherness in the encounter. One can not bend over backwards to see the faith of the other if one has lost the surety of one's own footing.

There is of course no doubt that Buddhist and Christian perceptions of one another's otherness can be mistaken. Insight is often biased by oversight that needs to be enlightened, and the dialogue requires constant vigilance in this regard. At the same time, blindspots in the way one tradition views itself are often transparent to the those who view it from the outside. The encounter with Buddhism, for example, has done a great deal to awaken Christianity to its own cultural colonialism in Buddhist lands, just as Christian concerns with liberation has given Buddhists serious cause to reflect on its own tendencies to remove the virtue of compassion to such a level of abstraction or privatization that it is no longer concerned with producing norms of what is morally acceptable in the spheres of their own cultural influence.

Apart from this critical function, the dialogue is also an experiment in rethinking the self-understanding of the participating traditions. The Christian looks through the lens of Buddhist faith to have a second look at Christian faith; the Buddhist looks through the lens of Christianity to look again at Buddhist faith. And both sides talk about what it is they see, generating questions for further reflection. Intellectual conscience and deference to the history of the development of doctrine demand that these questions not harden into new positions without first being returned to the living context of one's own faith. The kinds of questions raised in this re-visioning are often disturbing, but on further reflection often turn out to be positions once dismissed as irrelevant, untenable, or heretical. What if the creator God were impersonal? What if the saving Dharma were personal? In allowing such questions to arise and be taken seriously, the interreligious dialogue demands not only an openness to another's view of one's own faith, but an openness to reevaluating the doctrinal pluralism in one's own past.

If this change of heart toward one's own past is not to become a mere intellectual curio for specialists, a complimentary conversion is required towards the positive role that another faith has to play in one's own faith today. This is the greatest challenge of the dialogue insofar as it nudges the dialogue out of itself and into the world of living religious belief and practice, where the orientation to mission and to vernacular culture must now find a way to convert an interreligious world. I repeat: it is not a question of Buddhism and Christianity simply sharing with one another techniques of proselytizing their respective affiliates; nor is it merely a matter of leading those who have strayed from religious affiliation back into one or the other fold. It is a question of converting Buddhism to Christianity and Christianity to Buddhism.

The idea of mutual, interreligious conversion is far from clearly defined. In the context of the dialogue itself, it is still no more than the hint of an inspiration whose faint breath one feels cross the cheek from time to time. There are numerous instances of cross-fertilization in doctrinal understanding, and these can be documented in print and discussed formally.[10] But the real test— whether any of this is *useful* to personal belief and to the exercise of faith in action—is harder to devise. Here again, I would stress that the richest harvest of the dialogue lies outside the forum of dialogue itself, in the faith of ordinary believers. A good example of what mutual conversion might mean rises from the very real question of the cross-cultural transplanting of Christianity and Buddhism to one another's cultural spheres.

For all the havoc that secularization has worked on the established churches in Judeo-Christian lands, the cultural roots of church and secular society are inextricably bound up with one another. Even the most anti-religious ideologues drink from the same wells as those who uphold traditional Christianity. It is no more possible to uproot language, custom, modes of thought and morality from Christianity than it would have been possible for Christianity to take hold in Europe had it not been nourished in the very soil of the paganism it set out to overturn. The same may be said of Buddhism in countries like Japan, Korea, Thailand, Vietnam, and even China, where religion, irreligion, and anti-religion can only be set off against one another because of the vastness of their commonalties.

In such circumstances, the work of religious conversion, far from starting with a cultural *tabula rasa,* has a solid, even if largely unreflected, base from which to begin. It is another thing when it comes to spreading Buddhist teachings in traditional Christian cultures or vice-versa. By and large, the missions of both religions have resigned themselves to teaching new proseltyes to speak a strange language, behave in strange customs, think in strange patterns, and adjust to strange art, architecture, and music—and then hope that in time the strangeness will wear off and become culturally acceptable. Not that this is an altogether unreasonable hope, since living cultures are always adjusting at the fringes to what is foreign; and it is of this manifold of adjustments that some of them sink into common use with time. The problem for Buddhism and Christianity is that in the process of honoring their missionary orientation, they dishonor the accompanying orientation to vernacular culture.

The interreligious dialogue's concern with mutual conversion obliges us to think of the alternative: What would happen to

Christianity if popular Buddhist culture were accepted as the foundation for Christian faith? And what would happen to Buddhism in non-Buddhist lands if it embraced as its own religious ground what is fundamentally a Christian culture? What would it be like for a Christian missioner to introduce the teachings of Jesus by way of the unconscious religious modes of thought and value that flow in the life's blood of a Buddhist country? Or for a Buddhist missioner to preach the Dharma through Christian conventions?

The questions are far from rhetorical. Perhaps the clearest idea we have of what it would "be like" is the history of how each of these religions at their origins absorbed the religious atmosphere and customs of their own time in order to take root. Traditions become proud as they become more widespread, more intelligent, and institutionally stronger; and this pride makes it difficult to recognize the possibility of needing to return to the humility of their birth. No doubt there are other ways less menacing to the integrity of tradition for religions to claim one another's wealth. The only sure way to avoid the risk of distorting one's own religious tradition in dialogue with those of another is to forego the dialogue altogether. This does not mean that the interreligious dialogue encourages indifference to the fate of tradition. On the contrary, only a firm commitment to tradition can generate the sort of radical "kenosis" of the past that can give credence to the hope, born on the forum of dialogue but destined to transform religion in our times, of Buddhism and Christianity converting to one another's truth.

NOTES

[1] Mt. 28:19; see Mk. 16:16, Lk. 24:47.

[2] The comment was made by D. S. Cairns, chairman of the commission for dealing with non-Christian religions. It is cited in W. H. T. Gairdner, *Edinburgh 1910: An Account and Interpretation of the World Missionary Conference*. Published for the Committee of the World Missionary Conference (Edinburgh and London: Oliphant, Anderson & Ferrier, 1910), 281.

³ *Mahāvagga*, 1.11–12.

⁴ *Rock Edict* 13.

⁵ Clarence H. Hamilton, "Buddhism," in H. F. McNair, *China* (Berkeley: University of California Press, 1946), 297. See also Joseph Kitagawa, *Religions of the East* (Philadelphia: Westminster Press, 1968), 188–221.

⁶ Acts 2.

⁷ *Cullavagga* 5.33.1

⁸ See references in Franklin Edgerton, *Buddhist Hybrid Sanskrit Grammar and Dictionary* (Delhi: Motilal Banarsidass, 1977), 2.

⁹ Jan Van Bragt, 諸宗教対話の諸問題 ["Problems in Interreligious Dialogue"] in 宗教と文化 [*Religion and Culture*], ed. by the Nanzan Institute for Religion and Culture (Kyoto: Jinbun Shoin, 1994), 45.

¹⁰ Perhaps nowhere is this discussed more forthrightly than in John B. Cobb, Jr.'s *Beyond Dialogue: Toward a Mututal Transformation of Christianity and Buddhism* (Philadelphia: Fortress Press, 1982). To the best of my knowledge, none of Prof. Cobb's many Buddhist colleagues in the dialogue has produced a document of conversion to Christianity comparable to Cobb's account of how Buddhism has changed him and how he thinks Buddhism might change through Christian influence.

Interreligiosity
and Conversion

In the late summer of 1996 the research staffs of the Nanzan Institute for Religion and Culture and the Institute for Oriental Philosophy gathered for a symposium on "Catholicism and Sōka Gakkai." The event concluded a year of colloquia and discussions held at the two centers and was published in the following spring. The book quickly went to a second printing and focused considerable attention on the first efforts of a small circle of scholars within Sōka Gakkai to step away from their religion's traditionally exclusivistic stance and enter into dialogue with scholars of another religion. To date, the whole venture has met with a polite but unintimidating silence from institutional authorities of the Buddhist movement.

In preparing an opening Orientation address for the symposium, I had in mind the numerous Christian scholars who had warned us of mixing publicly with Sōka Gakkai, a group whose political chicanery at home and suspicious dealings abroad has given fuel to pulp journalism for the past two decades and more. Everything reminded me of the view held about the Christian churches in many parts of the Islamic world and even in certain mainstream currents of Southeast Asian Buddhism. But most of all I was reminded of the warning that Rudolf Harnack issued nearly a hundred years ago about comparing one religion's good theory with another's bad practice.

In any case, the burden of my opening remarks was to show, if only between the lines, that the scholarly dialogue must not allow itself to be dominated by the kinds of questions that preoccupy the encounter between religious establishments.

This lecture was subsequently published as「オリエンテーション,『カトリックと創価学会——信仰・制度・社会的実践』 [*Catholicism and Sōka Gakkai: Faith, Structures, Social Praxis*], ed. by the Nanzan Institute for Religion and Culture. Tokyo: Daisan Bunmeisha, 1996), 11–28. The English translation later appeared in the *Bulletin of the Nanzan Institute for Religion and Culture* 20 (1996): 19–30.

THE SYMPOSIUM THAT brings together today the Institute for Oriental Philosophy and the Nanzan Institute for Religion and Culture is the last in a series of meetings that began as something of an ambiguous adventure for all concerned. The shape and general focus of the discussions, which we decided on together in a joint consultation, was clear enough: members of the two research institutes would come together to discuss the meaning of belief, institutional structure, and social praxis in our respective traditions. In general the series of ten colloquia kept to this framework and produced an exchange of information, cleared up some misunderstandings, highlighted many points of contrast and was, by and large, fruitful as such things go.

Normally it would be my duty in this orientation to our closing symposium to lay out the guiding insights. But there is another agenda that must be addressed first, and one which was more present in this dialogue than at any other time in our past experience of dialogue with other religions in Japan.

From the start, all of us involved realized that there was a double-entendre to even the most overtly academic of our discussions. From Nanzan's side, this was the first time that we had attempted such discussions with a religious group originating in the twentieth century. In restricting ourselves in the past to the so-called "world religions," we were already at something novel enough. But to go the step further and take as our partner one of the "new" religions brought additional problems. For the Institute for Oriental Religions, the move was bolder still in that it represented a first concerted effort by scholars within the Sōka Gakkai to carry on a dialogue with their Christian counterparts.

This is the time to air openly what some of those problems were, and to look at them in the hindsight of the discussions and exchanges that actually took place.

I

To begin with, we were faced at Nanzan with the problem of which group to choose. On the one hand, any number of the new religions have actively solicited our participation, as individuals and as a research center, in local and international conferences. In many, if not most cases, these invitations did not stem from a scholarly tradition or academic caucus within these groups, but from public relations projects thinly disguised as academic interest. This is not to say that all such meetings are without all academic value, only that their primary focus was not the quest for understanding but a display of some other symbolic importance. All of this is not lost on the participating scholars who quickly see through it all (though the offer of free travel and accommodations may oblige them to a certain public silence), which leads me to suspect that the symbolic importance is more for those who do not attend the events—on the members of the sponsoring religious group and perhaps on the wider world of those who watch the activities of religions. In any case, this did not seem the right place to begin.

On the other hand, working as scholars, we have amicable relations with scholars of any number of new religions, including some that are not disposed to enter into religious dialogue with Christianity in Japan or elsewhere. In other words, whereas scholarly dialogue and cooperation have proceeded with individuals in these traditions, blind to differences of faith these many years, actual interfaith dialogue between their traditions and our own has not yet taken place or been out of the question. It was from this end of the spectrum that we felt our choice had to be made.

The problem was this: Given our own absence of formal dialogue in the past with the new religions, and given further the lack of dialogue among the new religions themselves at the academic level, would the selection of one partner be perceived as an endorsement of one group or an implicit critique of others? Would the "public relations" dimension enter in despite our good intentions and that of our actual partners? Would we run the risk of being used in the way that has become almost synonymous with certain new religious movements vis-à-vis Christianity, for purposes quite outside of the dialogue itself? For the fact is the presence of Catholic scholars engaged in dialogue can be, and often has been used as propaganda against the will of people just like ourselves.

Not to be overlooked in this regard was the obvious preoccupation with many new religions in Japan to be on friendly terms with the Vatican, and in particular to be singled out above other religions for special treatment. Even though we do not as such represent, by delegation, the Vatican, the world Catholic Church nor even the Catholic Church in Japan, the danger of our efforts being perceived as a political choice was there.

In this same connection, there was some fear that we would somehow approve, by entering into dialogue, many of the practices of forced proselytizing and violation of human rights for which certain of the new religions have been criticized by the Catholic Church. No matter that such criticism has not always been fair—the symbolic value of the dialogue could be misinterpreted easily by Catholics and Christians engaged in serious dialogue in Japan. Finally, there was some anxiety over taking a step naively in the direction of dialogue with a religion that may have left scars in the Christian community, or among those in the Buddhist traditions with which we have had a long-standing dialogue, of which we at the Nanzan Institute were unaware.

Clearly the reasons for sticking to classical and world religions were compelling. While I myself was determined not to let these fears cripple us, I have to admit that they were part of what went into our decision to seek a middle road, by entering into formal academic dialogue with what we considered a serious academic research center, and as far as possible to make this an interfaith dialogue among believers but among believers who come together as scholars.

Happily the Institute for Oriental Philosophy was of the same mind when we presented our proposal. Given the past relationships between the Catholic Church and the Sōka Gakkai, the plans proceeded smoothly in a way that none of us imagined would happen. In this way the inter-institute dialogue began.

From the side of the Institute for Oriental Philosophy there were no doubt anxieties, too. Most obvious is that the parent organization of the Institute, the Sōka Gakkai, had traditionally kept aloof from interfaith dialogue. The reasons for this have tended to be tacit or at least not widely publicized. Although I have a hard time finding any reasons I can sympathize with, it is not hard for me as a Catholic to find like reasons within our own tradition. For despite all the efforts that have been made at a fair and open dialogue with other religions, there are many who have opposed it, and continue to oppose it as apostasy, or who have tried to strategize it for the purposes of expansionism.

There is another factor that enters into the dialogue. The split of the lay members from the monastic Nichiren Shōshū has meant that structurally the Sōka Gakkai was going through a major upheaval for which it was hoped the Catholic experience might be of some help. In fact, the dwindling ranks of the clergy, the dramatic loss in esteem, and thinning out of the flocks of the traditional "pastorate" and the like, even in traditional Catholic countries, have in effect meant that many in the Catholic tradition have made that split on their own. In any case, the decision on the part of the Institute for Oriental Philosophy to enter into dialogue was a bold one that came from within their own members, not from the top down, and as such represents an act of courage and risk of censorship much like that of the predecessors of dialogue in our own Catholic tradition, on whose shoulders we stand for the freedoms we enjoy today.

And perhaps, too, under the surface of it all, was something of the widespread fear mentioned earlier that, when all is said and done, Catholics engage in dialogue as a mission strategy. The fear is not entirely paranoid. After all, the open-ended dialogue that we enjoy today was an outgrowth of a, for the time, rather liberal missiological stratagem circulating around the middle of the century known as "pre-evangelization." The idea was that one should look for preparatory signs of openness to Christianity in religions that do not know the Church or the gospel. Initially it was an audacious step, resisted by those who divided the world neatly into the faithful and the pagans. But the final goal was the same: conversion to the one true Church.

This attitude is still prevalent and has not escaped the attention of those who have been its object. (Indeed, the same methods are also apparent in new and lay Buddhist movements in predominantly Catholic cultures like those of South America and the Philippines.) The critique has been more forceful from quarters in the world of Islam, both because of the cultural agenda of the nineteenth-century missionary movement, only now coming to its end, and because of the current fundamentalist mood. As these critics view the interreligious dialogue, the absence of outright attempts to convert others to Christianity cloaks a more basic conversion to a certain idea of human relations and a certain way of being human—a humanism that has historically been the support of Christianity. This extends not only to the political and the economic realm, but also to the rational and religious dimension.

To put it briefly, the idea is that only a religion that is self-reflective and self-critical after the manner of Western theology is worthy of the human being at the end of the twentieth century. Thus, entering into dialogue means taking on this attitude, and in a sense is still a kind of "pre-evangelization." The closer non-Christian religions approach to methods of Christian theology, the more prepared they are to enter into the cutting edge of dialogue—but at the same time, the more likely they are to be absorbed into a language game at which Christianity has the edge of a long tradition and history. This is clearest in religions without a scripture or at least predominantly ritual, but it is also the case in religions based on non-European philosophical principles.

In Japan, this issue is close to the surface, and I should like to think it is so because the dialogue belongs to a broader trend in Christian theology of self-reflections on the Hellenic and Western biases of Christianity vis-à-vis Buddhism in particular. Indeed, the leading role that Japanese Christianity has played in interreligious dialogue is partly a function of its concern with facing up to its own failures to inculturate.

As our discussions progressed, these ambiguities wove in and out of one another until in the end everything came together in a day of closed-door discussions held at the Institute for Oriental Philosophy in Tokyo last July. It is because of those discussions that the matter can be aired here without animosity or fear of offense. It is a matter, ultimately, of common concern. In hindsight, I have no question but that Sōka Gakkai believers of the Institute for Oriental Religion were as fitting dialogue partners as we have ever had. I am also persuaded that the actual discussions and relationships that grew up outweighed and obscured the fears of either side using the other to its own advantage. This may in fact be the best answer to the suspicions, which cannot really be dealt with on their own. The proof of the dialogue was in the dialoguing.

II

Each of the major themes of the symposium—faith, structure, social praxis—will be given its own session. I would like to devote the rest of my comments to the question of the relationship between academic dialogue such as that we have been engaged in together as research institutes and the fact that we do so as members who belong to a particular religious tradition.

To begin with, I wish to state my own conviction concerning the religiosity of the interreligious dialogue itself. It seems to me that this business of getting together is not mere talk about religion, nor mere religious theory, but is itself a religious act. Contrary to the view that dialogue, like the scientific study of religion, requires stepping away from one's convictions in order to create an atmosphere of objectivity or at least etiquette, there are a range of convictions that are strengthened in the dialogue as no where else. In this connection, I would offer three comments.

1. *In laying out the motivations for entering into interfaith dialogue, however much one may cite scripture, documents, and the sayings of founders, saints, and sages in one's religious tradition, the core attitude of dialogue really belongs to the sound common sense that makes any reflection on the reality of religion today possible.*

The simple historical fact is that the advance of the scientific spirit in our own century has accomplished far more than centuries of religious teachings, theology, and philosophy were able to accomplish with regard to instilling tolerance for religious traditions other than one's own. It is no accident that those religions institutions and thinkers who have most resisted the progress of science are also those most averse to the consequences of religious pluralism. The scientific spirit rests on a conviction that whatever authority human reason has, rests on a continual interplay among the facts of experience, the irritation of doubt, and the release from this irritation by settling questions in open forum. Secular civilization has become dependent on this spirit, not only for the progress of its knowledge and technology, but also for a critique of that progress. Given the pluriformity of the human religious experience and expression, to enter into dialogue with one of another faith requires no more than a modicum of good will and a moment's consultation with that common sense. To refuse to do so on principle, even religiously motivated principle, is an offense to reasonableness.

I would go further and claim that ultimately the refusal to place one's own faith in an interreligious context of dialogue cannot reasonably be grounded on religious belief or special revelation, but rests on a decision to cling to one's own opinions and absolve them from their wider context. This means not just clinging tenaciously to particular tenets, but clinging tenaciously to the opinion that this is the proper way to believe. This tenacity is no more a specifically religious act than liberation from it is. It is at direct odds with the social impulse of our human nature, as the openness to truth is a confirmation of our nature. The same holds true in the case of an institution that sees moral authority as a way to settle matters of truth a priori, oblivious of the pluriformity of experience and the community of thinkers. Any reason that rejects self-criticism, again however religiously expressed its motivations and grounds, is at odds with common sense and humanity. Realizing this is the beginning of dialogue.

In our discussions, there were any number of points at which allegiance to one's respective religious bodies came into question. At times these counterpositions were justified as belonging to a "minority view" within the wider tradition. Such justification, it seems to me, only makes sense if one accepts the claim of moral authority to fix the majority view and to proscribe rational doubt in favor of tenacity to fixed beliefs. In the context of dialogue, the negative sense of a "minority view" departing from the mainstream of tradition is out of place. On the contrary, insofar as the forum of dialogue is truly open, such wrestling with received tradition and free exchange of opinion is not suspect but rather the proof of the humanity of our religious reflection. That having been said, there is a second factor to consider at once:

> 2. *Interreligious dialogue cannot ignore the moral dimension of the fact that religions have always fostered an admiration for the person who can dismiss reason in favor of submission to the authority of tradition and of the strength, simplicity, and directness of tenacity to one's beliefs.*

Because authority and tenacity are tied more directly to moral action than is scientific method or the radical search for truth, religions have tended to define themsleves at the limits of reason. There is something in our nature that admires the moral goodness of the believer as somehow outweighing the renunciations of rational thinking. In the context of interreligious dialogue, which is a rational process, however, insistence on speaking from a standpoint of faith is less an argument for authority than it is an expression of the conviction that the moral impulse is an essential ingredient to a religious outlook and life. In our discussions, there was a sense emerging that moral concerns were not merely the concretization or social consequences of the founding ideals, teachings, traditional institutions, even personal faith of a religion, but belonged to the primary core of religion.

   3. *Interreligious dialogue is not about pitting the particular symbols of faith against one another in order to compare their relative merits and demerits, but about a mutual conversion.*

By conversion I mean articulating in mutually understandable language a view of life based on those symbols, a sense of how the evolution of one's own symbolic system is enriched and challenged by that of other faiths, and a joint attempt to decide what is morally acceptable in the social sphere and what is not. It is here that the dialogue becomes properly a religious act.

   In this sense, dialogue requires a change in the way individual religions have classically thought of truth. As long as the unshakable, nonevolutionary, solid foundation of faith is a special revelation chiseled in stone, giving access to facts about the universe not otherwise accessible, then dialogue about religious truth can only be political etiquette or pre-evangelical strategy. What is needed is a conversion to a kind of dual-affiliation. In the same way that one may feel oneself a primary citizen of the world and a secondary citizen of one's own particular culture, so, too, one's primary religious allegiance can be the point at which religious faiths together open out to responsibility for the world, and the secondary allegiance to that concrete set of symbols or revelations within which one lives and thinks. This standpoint of dialogue, on which only in joining the two loyalties can one think of truth and act the truth, though not limited to formal dialogue, must be present.

   In saying that my particular religious affiliation is secondary, I do not mean that it is dispensable. In fact, its indispensability is the deepest mystery of religion: that our specific symbolic system is not exhausted or reducible to any general religious principles or insights, but remains a sine qua non of religious discourse. Like the senses without which we cannot take in the world, still it is not the senses but the world that is primary. Similarly, one cannot be a citizen of the world, picking and choosing what one finds of benefit in many cultures and languages, without a grounding in one language and culture. My Christianity is my vernacular language without which I am silent in the dialogue.

In this same regard, I would note that the "suitability" of a partner for dialogue is ultimately not directly a matter of relative institutional strengths. This is because finally dialogue does not take place between institutions—theological or ritual traditions, financial conglomerates, political regimes—but between those never quite worthy representative individuals who in some measure accept responsibility for the continuation of those institutions. There is no question of a lack of parity in dialogue simply because of a disparity in the length of one's history, the indigenousness of one's presence, the presence or absence of a scriptural tradition or priesthood, or even the size of one's membership. In the case of the Sōka Gakkai and Christianity, it is clear that the Catholic Church is worldwide the institutionally stronger, but inside Japan those roles are reversed.

Such dialogue does not take place between mere individuals, but representative ones, that is, individuals who do not rely merely on their own insight and reflection but recognize as critical the limits imposed on self-understanding and self-determination by past and present circumstances. The constant reference to our respective history and ongoing change was not a distraction, but a necessary ingredient of what we were trying to do. Successful dialogue is a religious attitude of mind that builds up a community of faith that cuts across traditional lines, a community which is through and through religious and whose cooperation is all the more important because it is not institutionalized.

Mutual conversion takes place in a community of faith united against the bad habit of what Rudolf Harnack called "comparing one religion's good theory with another's bad practice." Although this kind of reasoning is not to be discounted in a fair number of conversions of individuals from one faith to another, the sensible thing in the dialogue is to try to find a harmony between one's own theories and one's own practice. This is a common quest that only proceeds better if one can secure the help of others.

This question of mutual conversion through dialogue to a kind of interreligiosity and its broader idea of religious truth did not come up directly in the year's discussions. In another sense, the question of a broadening of religious loyalties beyond one's particular affiliation and awakening to the need of mutual support for moral praxis was there beneath the surface all along. In conclusion, I would like to address this matter in more specific terms.

III

The very idea of "conversion" implies both an awakening to reality and a readjustment of habits of behavior. To say that conversion is "mutual" does not mean that it is a kind of joint statement or joint action after the manner of a treaty or contract, but that each side is intimately involved in the process of change of the other. This is not only a personal matter, but one that affects the structure of religious institutions. I would like to single out six points of orientation towards conversion that directly engage the religious establishment interreligiously, including of course Catholicism and the Sōka Gakkai.

Each of these orientations is motivated not only by the time-worn nobility of ideals to be found in religious traditions everywhere, but also by the persistent ignobility of the failure of organized religion to measure up to them. Together they suggest that part of the purpose of cultivating the disciplines of interreligious dialogue is to protect religious activity from yielding to its dark side. The longer religious institutions join in dialogue not only to exchange information but to participate in a religious activity that affects the way a religious body conducts itself in history, the more apparent the perils of isolating one religious tradition from another become. The case of Aum Shinrikyō is a grotesque example of what can happen when one religious body deliberately distances itself from the community of other religious bodies. As its leadership lost touch with religious ideals and become hopelessly entangled in the shadows of economic and political agenda, the piety of its rank-and-file membership was enlisted in the service of the worst kind of social destructiveness. As extreme as the consequences were, the bare *pattern* of the process is not unfamiliar to the history of religion. Missionary tactics of persuasion by financial or institutional impressiveness, moral pressures to comply without question to institutional decisions, cultural imperialism, political extortion, and the like are all familiar weapons to the traditions of Catholicism and the Sōka Gakkai. My point here is that interreligious dialogue cannot get very far without obliging participants to face these perennial problems in the concrete in the light of our respective ideals and scriptures. In this connection, I would note that if there is one distinctive element that the Christian tradition has brought to dialogue with other religions, it is the willingness to face up to the inherent sinfulness of our institutions, and the willingness to see the correction or failure to correct as something that affects the role of religion within society as a whole. If it is not out of place for me to say so, this is an attitude that our Buddhist counterparts in general, including Buddhist groups like the Sōka Gakkai, have yet to accept as fully in the dialogue. That having been said, I take up the points of orientation to interreligious conversion.

First, the dialogue is oriented to improving our understanding and appreciation of the broader religious history of humanity. If there is, as I believe, a sense in which religious believers today can claim as their rightful inheritance the full wealth of religious insight, this requires a deliberate effort to make that inheritance better known. In taking this as a task of dialogue, the implication is that the truth and self-understanding of a religious way is best learned from one who believes and practices it, not from one who does not, which means recognizing the need to expose the faithful of one tradition to the teachers of another. In other words, if the dialogue is a religious act, and not merely an area of expertise for specialists, its religiosity must not become the special privilege of a select body of experts. It needs to become a permanent feature of the way we pass our respective traditions on from one generation to the next.

Second, the dialogical state of mind is oriented towards calming hostilities among religions of a size and power that makes them capable of generating, inspiring, or otherwise supporting warfare. This was one of the guiding ideas behind the call for a "global ethic" that featured prominently in the Parliament of the World's Religions held in Chicago last year. While the number of religious traditions to whom this applies is rather restricted, their institutional strength is such as to immunize them from the critique of smaller, less "developed" religious traditions. It may well be that when institutions—even religious institutions based on ideas of simplicity, peace, and equality—cross a certain threshold in size and wealth that they cannot avoid engagement in the area of political and economic warfare. If that is so, the promotion of peace by individual believers within these institutions, and the advance of interreligious contact with smaller religious ways not so compromised becomes crucial. In warfare as in so many other areas, it is naive to entrust the execution of a global ethic to the most powerful global institutions. The dialogue among religions must work to awaken religious establishments to this insight.

Third, dialogue is oriented towards ecumenism with factions, denominations, and sects that make up one's primary religious affiliation. Christian ecumenism has made great advances in the past fifty years, and the signs of ecumenical cooperation among Buddhists of different countries and persuasions are encouraging. In contrast, contact among the new Christian groups, beginning with those that grew up in the latter half of the last century, is wanting. The same animosities and competitiveness that keep them apart are also apparent in the new Buddhist groups of the far East. In the case of Japan, for example, while many of these groups fall over one another to enter into dialogue with non-Buddhist religions, they cannot suffer dialogue with their fellow Buddhists. I am persuaded that without progress in intra-religious ecumenism, there is no hope of the gains that Buddhism and

Christianity make in academic dialogue ever touching the soul of our age.

Fourth, dialogue is oriented towards the promotion of religious pluralism. Contrary to what dialogue might look like from the outside—and where established religion is concerned, let it be remembered, dialogue is still widely viewed as an esoteric activity—it does not take the question of doctrinal foundations lightly. Quite the opposite, it thinks about these questions all the time. And precisely because it does so in an interreligious context, it cannot but raise questions of the cultural and historical bias built into doctrinal understanding. The more one is made to understand the specificity of one's own religious way in the broader context of the religious history of the world, the more one is also driven to esteem pluralism and variety within one's own chosen faith. This is an important, even essential, by-product of dialogue among religions. At the same time, the pursuit of doctrinal questions in a context of dialogal openness can always lead to a change of affiliation for some individuals. Though this occurs less frequently than might be imagined, it is a sign of the health and honesty of the dialogue that such conversions occur from time to time: Christians becoming Buddhists, Buddhists becoming Christians, Christians and Buddhists of one denomination shifting to another. Insofar as such persons carry their commitment to dialogue with them, they may render a service to the religion they have "left" that perhaps no one else can render.

Fifth, the dialogue is oriented not towards an elimination of all proselytizing and teaching of one's own faith, but to a conversion of the means of expansion. In the same way that the end of the colonial age did not mean an end to the spread of particular languages and cultures throughout the world, so, too, the religions must consider, in dialogue, new ways to reach the whole world with their teachings. In the case of the Catholic tradition, missiological theory is still bogged down in the last century, but a recognition of the "pre-evangelical" truth of other religions for the teaching of Christianity coupled with a recognition of the pre-evangelical truth of Christianity for other religions is essential if we are to flourish in a pluralistic, interreligious world. In the same way that Christian teachings will never reach the soul of Japan without building on the indigenous religiosity of its people, neither will Buddhist groups active in the West really reach the soul of the West without an understanding of very different religious roots. To see these processes as something to encourage rather than as a competition to fear is a task that awaits interreligious dialogue in the years ahead.

Sixth and finally, the dialogue is oriented towards a conversion of self-understanding through a mutual engagement in one another's sacred texts. In addition to mutual reflection at the level of moral praxis, there is also a need to encourage more Buddhist readings of Christian scriptures, and vice-versa. This in turn requires a change of heart regarding the "authority" over the textual tradition. If we grant that the believing Christian, for example, can enter into the spirit of the New Testament in a way that the scholar who abstains from faith in order to be objective cannot, and that both together are necessary for "understanding" the scriptures, then might there not be a sense in which the believing Buddhist can further complement our understanding by reading the text with the eyes of another faith? Conversely, might not the Christian sensitivities enlighten Buddhist sūtras in a way instructive for the Buddhist believer? Emotionally, the possibility of being instructed in one's own faith by those in another is difficult to accept. Still, until such a conversion has been made, the religious dimension of the dialogue can never be complete.

Six Sūtras on the Dialogue
among Religions

In the year 2000 the Nanzan Institute for Religion and Culture celebrated the twenty-fifth anniversary of its formal foundation. To commemorate the occasion, we solicited papers for a special collection from current and former members of the staff. What follows is my contribution.

It had long seemed to me that the ever-growing library of theological materials on the nature, rules, and spirituality of interreligious dialogue was more of a nuisance to the actual business of dialogue than it was a help. As much as I disliked the idea of adding another essay on what dialogue is and what it means, I felt it was time to set aside my bias and clarify my own mind on the matter.

In particular, there were two fundamental points that seemed to me to be lacking in the literature as I knew it. First, that in laying out the motivations for entering into interfaith dialogue, however much one may cite scripture, documents, and the sayings of founders, saints, and sages in one's religious tradition, the core attitude of dialogue really belongs to the sound common sense that makes any reflection on the reality of religion today possible. And second, that interreligious dialogue is not about pitting the particular symbols of faith against one another in order to compare their relative merits and demerits, but about a mutual conversion.

Against this background, I tried to unravel six

139

threads from the complex of motivations, sentiments, and ideas that had motived the work of the Nanzan Institute and others like it.

Originally published as「宗教と宗教の対話についての六経」『宗教と宗教の《あいだ》』[Between religion and religion], ed. by the Nanzan Institute for Religion and Culture (Nagoya: Fūbaisha, 2000), 362–78.

PROOF OF THE importance of dialogue among religions does not have to be given here. To those engaged in it, the proof is in the experience. To those who need convincing by rational argument, there is a whole literature on the subject available in an array of languages. To those whose experience or convictions have led them to think otherwise, nothing I have to say here is likely to persuade them to change their minds on the matter. My concern here is of another sort.

That said, it is not always obvious to me that the advocates and critics of dialogue are talking about the same thing. This is not a lament; it is very much in the nature of dialogue that this be so. There is no corral into which one can herd a certain class of ideas and activities to brand them as belonging to the concept of dialogue. Nor is there any privileged height from which one can look down on the interactions among religion and generalize definitions or norms. Everything we say about dialogue—even in its most rational forms—has to be said within the whole confusing thick of it. It not a certifiable professional skill exercised in committee and answerable to some higher authority. It is an adventure of ideas.

Experience quickly teaches one that what happens when different religious ways encounter one another through the colloquia of their living believers rarely caters to the expectations and predictions of the participants. The results are more often haphazard and fragmentary than they are systematic. The greatest impact is more often felt in an arresting twist of a familiar idea, a neglected fact, an unanticipated sentiment, than in a deliberated consensus or clarification of differences.

This does not mean that the forum into which those of different religious traditions step to discuss matters of common concern is little more than a friendly chat over a neighbor's fence. It means only that in the meeting of religions, the greatest fruits of even the most rigorous and disciplined colloquium tend to bud in the spaces between the clash and clamor of ideas and intellectual tools, only to blossom and mature at another time and place, often with no visible sign of their origin.

This is all well and good for particular dialogues, but when it comes to talking about the whole dialogue enterprise as such and assessing its proprieties and improprieties, one longs for some kind of definition of terms. If indeed there *is* some transformation of perspective going on, and if it is indeed part of a wider shift in religious consciousness, then we want to be able to pause from time to time to see that it is not illusory or self-deceptive. To fail to do so is to leave oneself open to the sway of hidden agenda or naïve conformity to fashionable ideas, or to the simple conquest of one set of certitudes by another.

So we have two interlacing questions here. First, we need some parameters to delimit what we mean by interreligious dialogue; and second, we need to give some account of what makes a dialogue true to itself and what falsifies it.

Regarding the first, I trust the reader will not think it immodest of me if I take the occasion of the twenty-fifth anniversary of the founding of the Nanzan Institute for Religion and Culture to characterize the interreligious dialogue for the sake of this essay as *at least what the Nanzan Institute has been up to*. One could as well say, perhaps with more humility and less risk of begging the question, that the role we have played in the dialogue is no more than one facet of the multifaceted and still growing phenomenon.

My focus here, however, requires a bolder statement of the assumption that our experience counts for something in the wider story of the dialogue. I am obviously too much part of the phenomenon to claim any but the loosest form of objectivity in this regard, but insofar as the Nanzan Institute was established as a center for interreligious dialogue and has conducted itself for a quarter of a century with that aim in mind, and insofar as this conduct coincides with what is perhaps the longest continuous effort in human history to bring religions into dialogue with one another, then it seems fair to claim our own history as in some measure representative of an indispensable part of the dialogue.

Our own share in the adventure has been an intellectual one. I find no reason to parry criticisms that religions are much more than their doctrine or rational self-understanding, and that a dialogue centered on texts and ideas and bound to the principles of rational discourse is one-sided. Indeed, the wider network of interreligious activities that we have shared in within Japan and Asia and around the world has made it plain that ours is only one pattern woven into a much vaster tapestry. But the intellectual dialogue has been our part in the story, and I prefer to speak from what I have seen and heard, even though it bias some of the generalizations that follow.

Interreligious dialogue on the intellectual forum is dialogue in the most literal sense of the term: persons of one religious belief conversing with those of another. Although the setting is defined by the demands of rational argument, it is motivated by a desire that is anything but purely rational, namely the desire to understand better the religious dimension of the human in all its diversity. The focus of the conversation is variable, as is the format, but the pure and simple intention of helping each other to think more clearly and better informed about something that belongs to all of us as part of our common nature remains the permanent, if somewhat elusive, ideal. What distinguishes the interreligious dialogue from the academic study of religion or the mere broadening of one's horizon of understanding is the belief that something more is at work in religious understanding itself than the exercise of reason over a certain class of phenomena—that has us more caught up in its unspeakableness than we can catch with our speech. The mind of dialogue is wrapped in what we may call, *ignotium per ignotius,* mystery. This, at least, is the standpoint from which I have framed the remarks that follow.

At the same time, I freely admit that the kind of interreligious dialogue we have enjoyed at Nanzan qualifies as a luxury item when set against the backdrop of the way the world goes. For all the progress civilization has made in the tools it uses to work, to communicate, and to entertain itself, there is every indication that the quality of those basic cultural activities has deteriorated, that there seems to be an inverse correlation between the sophistication of our tools and the distribution of the wealth that gives access to them, and that organized religion seems by and large to have made peace with the contradiction to its principles. To step on to the forum of free dialogue uninhibited by direct responsibility to the world order is a privilege, the only possible justification for whose exercise is what happens in the history around the dialogue. This, too, I have in mind in what follows.

Regarding the second question of assessing the truthfulness of the intellectual interreligious dialogue, I would like to offer a number of propositions in the form of strands for weaving into the larger tapestry of the encounter among religions. By themselves these strands—or to use the Sanskrit term, sūtras—are slender and easily snap under the pull of the shuttle. They need to be braided together to be worked on the loom. By this I do not mean to offer a systematic methodology, let alone a set of norms for all intellectual dialogue among religions. I only wish to lay out one set of reflections regarding the question of what makes a dialogue true to itself, reflections phrased moreover from the standpoint of a Christian participant.

Others of the community of scholars who have made up the Nanzan Institute would no doubt phrase things differently and place the accent elsewhere. They may even take cause with some of these statements. We have been far too motley a crew to pretend anything more than a common orientation. The mistakes and oversights that have accompanied us along the way also belong to the story, but I shall leave them aside here. My idea is to wander between the lines of the history of the Institute in search of the spirit of dialogue that it has been our aim to serve.

Sūtra 1. **The spirit of interreligious dialogue need not be born of tradition in order to be reborn there.**

When Christianity encounters other religions today, it does so with a clear edge on the literature about dialogue. There is nothing in any other religion of the world to compare with the amount of theological reflection on the subject we find scattered across the Christian world. Nevertheless, it is necessary to disavow the claim that the primary inspiration to dialogue with the religions of Japan—Shinto, Buddhist, folk religion, and new religious movements—or indeed elsewhere, was born of the scripture or magisteria of my own tradition. (Nor do I find any evidence that any of the partners we have had could make such a claim on behalf of their own tradition.) If anything, the pioneers of dialogue had to contend at every turn with a barrage of scriptural passages and traditional beliefs that censured them for what they were doing.

In the case of the Nanzan Institute, the air had already cleared by the time the spade dug into the earth to break ground for the buildings. This reversal of fortunes that has brought the dialogue into the forefront of theological reflection and lent the weight of tradition to the effort frequently gives the impression that the dialogue is a distinctively Christian adventure. The facts of the matter are more humbling.

Christianity did not set out on its own initiative to dialogue with the great religions of the world. A few farsighted people saw a change taking place in secular consciousness regarding the promise of religious diversity, recognized it as something of spiritual importance, entered into it against opposition, and persevered until the time would come when the religious establishment itself would take credit for the spirit of dialogue in the name of its own perennial heritage. When the Second Vatican Council made its pronouncements on openness to non-Christian religions and religious free-dom—all rather tame by today's standards—it was not *initi-ating* a change of heart but *acknowledging* its presence. This recognition no doubt marked a watershed in the history of dialogue, siding with those who had cleared a way for Chris-tians to recognize truth in other religious ways.

If Christianity had to catch up with the saeculum in accepting the challenge of religious diversity, it now finds itself in the vanguard in significant numbers. It is not the absence of persecution that is the greatest proof that the spirit of dialogue has been reborn in Christianity. It is rather the reinterpretation of religious tradition to explain the openness to other faiths as a natural consequence of our own faith. Neglected figures of the past whose ideas on dialogue had been marginalized are now brought forth to center stage with pride. There is no reason to accuse theologians of historical revisionism; this is the way religious traditions have always tended to work.

Far more important for Christianity, and indeed for any other religion, than the fact that the dialogue was not born directly of its own tradition is the fact that it is being *reborn* there, that that the weight of an ancient tradition is now put *behind* the efforts of an idea of such far-reaching importance for the human community as a whole, instead of being made to stand *in front* of them like a barrier. And insofar as this can lead other religious ways to emulate the search for that spirit in their own traditions, the value of the rebirth is only enhanced.

Sūtra 2. **Dialogue is primarily a minority enterprise that stands free of the obligations of institutional religion.**

To applaud the encouragement that the religious establishment gives to the dialogue in general is not to say that the presence of religious institutions is essential to the dialogue at all levels. This is clearly the case with the intellectual dialogue, our focus here. To stand on the forum of dialogue is to stand as one professing a particular faith, and in that sense to stand as a representative of that faith, however wide or narrow the range of knowledge one brings. But it is not to stand as a representative of the institutional demands of that faith. The work of dialogue flourishes best when it stands free of the demands of official institutions.

Put the other way around, the representation of institutional concerns and policies tends more to inhibit the freedom of thought that is the soul of intellectual dialogue. One does not leave one's faith at the door, but one does leave the bulk of religion there—including the dimension of institutional obligations.

At the same time as concrete obligations vis-à-vis institutional religion are left out of the dialogue, the idea of institutional religion can never be far away from the talk of religion. Even at its most ethereal doctrinal heights, religious discourse is embedded in history as much through its visible political and economic structures as through the consciousness of its individual believers. Discourse and history are always correlative. But in the same way that private religious experience, for all its importance, cannot be a subject of rational discussion unless it be abstracted from the experiencing subject, so, too, the concerns of maintaining religious structures need to be abstracted to their ideal if they are to be discussed at all. From the standpoint of institutional religion, then, the dialogue is always and ever a minority enterprise, unsuited to the full demands of a religious tradition.

Sūtra 3. **The dialogue's purpose relies on being purposeless.**

In the Christian world, dialogue commissions and courses have helped to find the enterprise a place in the academic and ecclesial establishment around the world. The phenomenon is especially noticeable in Christianity, but happily not only there. As significant as this development is, it does not entail the conclusion that the dialogue itself, especially the intellectual dialogue, should be shouldered with agenda outside the dialogue, whether directly related to the religious establishment or not. The temptation to do so is enormous.

One thinks, for example, of initiatives to link the dialogue among religions to some form of "global ethic." The aim of prompting among those of the world's religions engaged in warfare as an important step to world peace is laudable enough in its own right, as is the collaboration among religions to counter systematic infringements on human rights and structural injustice. Such agenda understand dialogue as a form of lobby or task force, differing from the dialogue among nations and corporations in terms of motivation but not in terms of structure. But this does not imply that *all* dialogue must be fitted out with an agenda in order to be true to itself. On the contrary, I agree with my predecessor Jan Van Bragt that one of the defining aims of the intellectual dialogue is to be "without aim."[1]

The insistence on a form of dialogue forum free from secondary aims in no sense contradicts those aims. It only asserts that clarity of thought is *also* served by an environment that steps away from the pressing concerns of the present. There is no argument against the fact that such a retreat is powerless in the concrete, lacking an orientation towards history. To say that such things are not its immediate concern is not to say that these are not concerns that the dialogue may, on some other forum, serve. In other words, the claim to purposeless can only be upheld if one sees the dialogue forum as a deliberate but provisional ascesis. The intellectual dialogue is not a permanent state of religious identity or even of religious reflection. Dialogue does not aim at being the fullness of religious belief, let along of religious practice. Nor is it even a permanent "ingredient" in ordinary religious self-understanding. The forum of dialogue itself is ancillary to wider questions of historical identity and morality only because the activity of the forum is ancillary to nothing. Like play that loses its quality of play once made subservient to some purpose outside of the playing itself, the dialogue flourishes in its purposelessness.

For this same reason, it is a mistake to see engagement in dialogue as the work of trained specialists. Dialogue succeeds more as a result of experience than of expertise. Attempts to lay down specific "ground rules" for intelligent discourse among believers of different faiths inevitably generates a priesthood of experts to monitor the results of such encounters and assess their success or failure. To avoid this, one needs to understand the dialogue as a good in its own right whose purpose is to serve no other purpose.

Sūtra 4. Dialogue is selective of tradition and may even require a dispensing with tradition altogether.

When one doctrinal tradition meets another, there is no obligation to represent the entirety of the tradition into the picture. What would compromise one's integrity in discussions of theology or the comparative history of ideas—where the whole picture, or at least one perspective on it, is always potentially relevant—does not pose the same danger to interreligious dialogue. The question of God, for example, does not demand that the Christian implicate the doctrine of the trinity; when speaking of salvation, there may be no need to represent theories of the soul or final judgment. In framing a question for discussion in common, the number of details left in the penumbral shadows will be much wider when a Christian speaks to a Shinto, a Buddhist, or a Taoist than when he speaks to other Christians, and vice-versa. Indeed, nothing is more stifling in dialogue than the attempt to overwhelm the discussion with details out of a sense of loyalty to tradition. As long as the concern with clarity of thought about the religious dimension of the human is primary, the clarification of tradition will remain secondary. I have no doubt that this latter is important, and can even gain from interreligious discussion. I mean only to suggest that the dialogue is better served where participants are relieved of the obligation to the fullness of tradition. This ascesis is well known to those who join with other religious for social causes. I believe it also can have a place in intellectual dialogue.

As corollary to this, some mention should be made of the problem of fundamentalism. I do not happen to believe that doctrinal fundamentalism is an acceptable rational position, but neither do I believe that the only choice is to counter it with the same level of intolerance. Where theological and philosophical discussion are concerned, fundamentalism has no place at all. But in the dialogue among religious believers, the absence of appeal to differing doctrines, which are in principle rejected by the fundamentalist position, does not mark the end of dialogue. It is rather the ultimate test of its inner heart.

On the bare agreement that there is in us all a natural drive to know more of the mystery that envelops life, and that religious belief and practice is in some sense an attempt to respond to this drive, it should be possible to tolerate dispensing with doctrinal assertions specific to one's own faith in order to broaden the common ground of understanding, provided the conditions discussed in the other sutras expressed here are met with.

Although we tend to associate fundamentalism with an established and comprehensive standpoint, we are more likely to encounter it as a dimension of all articulated tradition. Here, too, the emphasis in dialogue must be on recovering a basic human religiosity from within fundamentalism, as the only possible healer of the wound of intolerance, not on asserting one's doctrinal loyalties at all cost.

Sūtra 5. The dialogue is a religious activity, but one that leads neither to religious conversion nor religious convergence.

On the one hand, critics of the intellectual dialogue, with its preference for the rule of logical discourse over the full representation of tradition and its distance from established institutions, often complain that the dialogue is a covert attempt to fuse existing religious traditions into one another at their points of contact. On the other hand, critics of the predominance of the Christian presence in the dialogue complain that it is a covert attempt to convert other religions to Christian doctrine or at least the Christian way of understanding doctrine.

The intellectual dialogue, as I have insisted above, is always more than a forum for intellectual debate or the exchange of information among knowledgeable experts. It is not merely *about* religion after the manner of the philosophy, psychology, sociology, or history of religion, but in an important sense is *itself* a religious act—an exercise of faith in its own right. This does not, however, necessitate a change of affiliation or any other attempt to adjust the previous institutional commitments of the individuals. The experience of dialogue can, of course, prompt a conversion from one established religion to another, or even simply a conversion away from an established religion. But such consequences are not the concern of the dialogue itself. They occur away from the forum of dialogue, in the fuller world of religious practice and tradition where the austere conditions of the dialogue do not hold sway.

At the same time, it must be admitted that within the parameters of the dialogue, differences of belief that separate one religious way from another are often ignored. In terms of

the interaction among different Christian churches engaged
with a religion like Buddhism, it is true that there is a mood of
spontaneous ecumenism that takes over and sets aside secondary concerns that would derail the whole function of a colloquium between religions. Although Buddhist sectarianism is
of a very different sort from that found in the Christian world,
and although the progress of an intra-Buddhist ecumenical
movement is still in its infant stages, this sectarianism is not
always relevant and often needs to be overlooked in the name
of clarifying some matter or other under discussion. There is
no reason in principle that this habit, common enough in the
intellectual dialogue, should carry over into the wider realm
of religious theory and practice, though neither is it impossible that some of what has been seen in the dialogue might
indeed carry over.

To repeat, the conditions of the dialogue neither generate
nor inhibit later decisions about erasing outdated sectarian
disjunctions or even the fusing of different religions in some
new form of religion. Such decisions require far more than
the tools of intellectual dialogue to be assessed, and the deliberate distancing from them in the dialogue only underlines
this fact.

In this regard, we do well to dispose here of the criticism
that Christianity, as a function of its monotheism, tends to
promote an exclusivism and a conflict among religions that is
foreign to the inveterate inclusivism and harmonious
approach of non-monotheistic eastern religions. In Japan, the
argument is used to support the claim that the spread of
Christianity, with its assumption that religion requires that
each individual affirm affiliation to one religion and disavow
affiliation with any other, is responsible for the policy of sepa-
rating Shinto and Buddhism inaugurated in the first year of
Meiji era. Further, it bolsters the claim that entering into
interreligious dialogue with Christianity involves a certain
imparity, given Christianity's inveterate tendency to erect
divisions in a form of religiosity that is naturally pluralistic.[2]

There are several problems with this argument, all of them surfacing in the dialogue. To begin with, contemporary Christianity is mightily divided on the question of pluralism, with those most active in the interreligious dialogue arguing the strongest case in favor of it. Far from promoting a cryptic form of exclusivism, Christianity in dialogue shows signs of healing itself of the exclusivism it has long clung to (or perhaps we might say as well, recovering a tolerance it had too long left on the periphery). Moreover, the clean separation of Christianity and eastern religions into the open and the closed risks committing the basic error that Harnack was fond of warning against: comparing one religion's theory with another's practice.[3] The pluralism that Christianity is claimed to disrupt exists religiously in the popular consciousness far more than it does among the doctrine of the institutional religions, for whom inclusivism is often littler more than a political or economic expediency.

At the same time, the pure monotheism that is said to foster exclusivism rarely exists in the popular Christian imagination, whose religiosity in practice is much closer phenomenologically to some form of polytheism than it is to high theology. The comparison is badly skewed from the start, and Christianity's efforts to open the tradition to dialogue is little served by this kind of misunderstanding.

Moreover, insofar as the forum of discussion with other religions serves Christian theology—or any other religion's method of doctrinal reflection for that matter—as an opportunity to propagate its own patterns of self-understanding as universal, it betrays the spirit of dialogue. Only in a heightened awareness of this tendency to partiality can different methods of self-understanding freely interact, clashing at one moment, borrowing at the next, persuading but always open to persuasion. This is the only form of transitive conversion in which the dialogue can be true to itself.

Sūtra 6. **At heart, Christianity is naturally Buddhist,**
     Buddhism is naturally Christian.

Tertullian's famous dictum *anima naturaliter christiana* has
traditionally been interpreted to mean that "the soul is naturally Christian," and hence that not to accept the Christian
faith is to rebel against what is in our nature. The Latin as well
as the original context of the phrase, however, suggests a radically different reading, one closer to the spirit of interreligious
dialogue. In the search for a point of contact between believers
and unbelievers, who lack a common scripture and teaching,
he appeals to the *testimonium animae:* In the deepest recesses
of the human heart the central ideas and symbols of Christianity are all to be found in a natural state. In other words,
"Christianity is natural to the soul." Christianity is not simply
a set of beliefs imposed from without by collective historical
forces or embraced in defiance of the desires of our human
nature. It is, at core, an expression of our nature.[4]

The consequence of this position is that Christianity is
also something natural to the soul of those who profess other
religions. To Christians experienced in the dialogue with
Buddhism in Japan this is patently evident. The other side of
the coin is that Christianity is not the only religion that can
make this claim. As the dialogue also attests, the Buddhist
path is natural not only to the Buddhist but to the Christian
as well—and not just to the small numbers of Christians who
step onto the forum of dialogue. The longer Buddhists and
Christians discuss with each other, the stronger grows the
sense in both of a fundamental, though often unexpected,
familiarity. If this were not the case, the dialogue would have
collapsed long ago or at least reshaped itself into a simple
intellectual exchange.

To say that Buddhism and Christianity are natural to the
soul is also to say that they are natural to one another. This
affinity is confirmed at the doctrinal level in the dialogue. As
Raimon Panikkar is fond of saying, religions are much like

languages. On the one hand, the languages of others sound like nonsense to those who do not speak them, and the peculiarities of one's own are unknown until one learns others. On the other hand, for all their difference there is no general idea in any language that cannot be understood in any other.[5] Only through the experience can one know what it means to say that a new language enriches the mind in general and the understanding of one's own language in particular.

Similarly, when the doctrinal expressions or scriptures of Buddhism are viewed through a Christian lens, or vice-versa, without including at the same time an expressed acknowledgment of the fundamental naturalness of the two religious ways to each other, and to the mind that tries to entertain them both in dialogue, they can only look like distortions. This awareness—one may call it a conversion to another religion in the intransitive sense, a metanoia without a loss of faith—in turn heightens the sensitivity to the richness of one's own religion's past, turning up equivalents and similarities in the most unexpected corners of the tradition.

Obviously there is a great deal in all historical religion that represents a lamentable imposition on the human spirit (and in some cases so overwhelming as to infect the religion as a whole). Neither Christianity nor Buddhism are clear of this charge. For any two religions to dialogue with each other, such things cannot be dismissed out of hand. Without the commitment to a basic natural affinity, however, the temptation for discussions of these matters to degenerate at some point into a contest is all but insurmountable.

There *are* forms of interreligious interaction that are measured in terms of winners and losers. War is one obvious example; conversion by proselytizing is another. The dialogue forum is not an arena; no one keeps score because there is no score to keep. It is rather, as I said at the outside, an adventure of ideas: seeing through the unique and distinctive qualities that sets one's own religious way off from others to the universal humanity beneath, and returning from that universal to have a second look at the unexplored potential of one own particularity.

The religious consciousness of the age that feeds the spirit of dialogue is not one attracted much to institutional religion as we have known it in the past. It picks and chooses from the sacred texts of the past, patches them together with modern texts, and stitches the whole together into a quilt of one's own design. This is a fabric of faith organized religion has always found dangerous, but it may also be the way the soul has always made sense of even the most dogmatic belief system in the midst of a world wider than the dogma. It also seems to point to radical changes in store for the world's great historical religions as we know them today.[6]

In any case, the spirit of dialogue which we have experimented with is certainly bigger than us and still blowing at our backs. We are its servants truly only if we protect ourselves from becoming its masters. This was the atmosphere into which I stepped over two decades ago, and which I find as fresh and challenging today as I did back then when Jan Van Bragt stood at the door and welcomed me in.

NOTES

[1] Jan Van Bragt,「諸宗教対話の諸問題」[Issues in Interreligious Dialogue], Nanzan Institute for Religion and Culture, ed.,『宗教と文化: 諸宗教の対話』 [*Religion and culture: The dialogue among religions*] (Kyoto: Jinbun Shoin, 1994, 45.

[2] For example, Yamaori Tetsuo, 山折哲男,「『宗教的対話』の虚妄性: 『宗教的共存』との対比において」[The deceptiveness of the "interreligious dialogue": A contrast with "religious coexistence"], *Religion and culture*, 83–96;『宗教の話』(Tokyo: Asahi Shinbunsha, 1997), 232–3.

[3] Cited in R. Otto, *India's Religion of Grace and Christianity Compared and Contrasted* (London: SCM Press, 1930), 59.

[4] In his *Apologia*, which was aimed at parrying criticisms of heretics and pagans, Tertullian uses the phrase only in passing in the first sense. It is

treated more fully in his *De testimonio animae,* where the second, more positive meaning, is in force.

[5] Raimon Panikkar, *La nueva inocencia* (Estella: Editorial Verbo Divino, 1993), 388.

6 See the essay "What Time Is It for Christianity?" later in this collection.

Christianity Today
The Transition to Disestablishment

*In the fall of 1996, I was invited to participate in a lecture
series on the state of the world's major religions today and
the prospects for their future. The event was sponsored by a
Buddhist association and aimed at the general Buddhist
public. I took the occasion to cast a sweeping view over the
history of Christianity as seen from the end of the twentieth
century, and from there to look at what seemed to me the
major conflicts facing Christian identity in the contemporary world.*

*I was later surprised to find that those who were selected
to represent Islam and Buddhism took positions much less
self-critical. Against that backdrop, my remarks were
received by some in the Christian world as unfair or at least
out of place. I was heartened, however, by the reception they
received by the organizers of the lecture series and by the
audience they had assembled. In particular, those belonging
to so-called "new religions" in Buddhism seemed envious of
the way in which Christianity has managed to accommodate self-criticism.*

*In an age marked by the intransigience of Church
authorities, I found the reaction strangely encouraging. At
the same time, not a few of my colleagues wrote with a sense
of relief that that I had opened my eyes in print to what had
really been obvious to so many of them for a long time.*

The lecture first appeared in print as「現代キリスト教の 行方
──脱制度化への推移──」『東洋哲学』[Oriental
Philosophy] 36/1 (1997): 21–48. The English translation reproduced here was published in *Inter Religio* 30 (Winter 1996):
63–79, and reprinted in *Dialogue* 24 (1997): 125-46 and in the
Journal of Oriental Studies 8 (1998): 38-58.

I HAVE BEEN asked to address you on the state of Christianity, a question which probably looks a lot simpler from the outside than it does from the inside. The more one is engaged in the events shaping the history of Christianity today, the more one is aware how fluid that history is, and how trying to sketch its portrait is like trying to paint on a flowing stream. In such circumstances, more important than cutting clear definitions is locating the most energetic points of change, and then trying to discern just where those changes are taking us. I assume that task this evening not as a representative *of* Christianity but only as one speaking *from* Christianity, and more particularly *from* the Catholic tradition. I insist on this distinction for two reasons.

First and most obvious, Christianity, even if restricted to its Catholic form, is too vast and too plural a phenomenon for an individual of so limited an experience as I to represent. The only honest representation is either that of a "symbolic personality" (as in the case of the pope of Rome) or a selection of delegates gathered in forum from around the world. In front of non-Christians, of course, Christians often set themselves up as representatives (the way an American, for instance, might present himself to a group of Japanese as an authority on American culture, or vice-versa), though this often amounts to little more than a way of stressing one's own belonging and the other's not-belonging. In front of their "own," few believers would dare to pose as representatives except for the smallest corner of the vast world of Christianity; nor can I bring myself to pose any differently before you. At the same time, I was raised within the Christian world and have no doubt absorbed a great deal of its influence—its virtues as well as its biases. Insofar as I have tried to reflect on this, I speak with some confidence as a representative from Catholic Christianity.

But there is a second reason why I decline to present myself as a representative of Christianity, and that is because I see the self-understanding of Christianity being shaken at its depths. At the surface of this deep groundswell, the loyalties of those who choose to identify with the institutional Church are divided between a "forward-looking" minority who welcome the change and a "backward-looking" majority who regret it. I will explain these terms later, but for now it is enough to remark that I wish to identify myself with the minority view and it is from that part of the tradition that I speak.

The tone of what I shall have to say, as I am only too aware, is in the key of *fin de siècle*, and to some extent shares in the mystique that the dawn of a new millennium works on us. It puts questions to us we might not otherwise think of, questions about our most treasured traditions and moral values, and perhaps, too, makes major upheavals seem more plausible than they might otherwise seem. I myself have no particular prophetic gifts, but the growing sense of readiness for prophecy is very much in my mind as I take a quick rush through Christian history in order to sketch for you an outline of the transition to disestablishment I see taking hold in Christianity today.

CHRISTIAN FASCINATION WITH THE MILLENNIUM

For Christians, movements greeting the end of the world or the dawn of a new age are nothing new. Already among the earliest disciples of Jesus we find the belief that the world would end within their own lifetime—a belief that found its way into the records of Jesus' own teachings. The postponement of the event to the "end of time" is echoed strongly in the visions of the Apocalypse, a book which has excited the imagination throughout Christianity's long history and given rise to the most outlandish predictions and interpretations of events in the secular world. Figures from Hitler to the pope of Rome to Henry Kissinger have been identified as the antichrist and the beast of the apocalypse.[1]

At the end of the twelfth century in Christian Europe, in the time of the Holy Roman Emperor Henry VI, a number of fanatical groups rose up proclaiming the dawn of a "Third Age." The idea was that after the First Age of the Old Testament (the Age of the Father, or Law) and the Second Age of the New Testament (the Age of the Son, or of Grace), the Age of the Spirit and of spiritual insight would escort history into its apotheosis. Behind it all stood a visionary named Joachim of Fiore (1135–1202), who had proclaimed the dawn of an *Ecclesia Spiritualis* which would usher in the age of John the evangelist and outlast the Church that traced its lineage back to Peter the apostle. At first encouraged by civil and Church authorities, Joachim was later condemned as a heretic, though others continued to revere him as a saint. His ideas on the movement of history were influential from the thirteenth to the sixteenth century. Witness the fact, for example, that fulfillment of his prophecy regarding two new spiritual orders that would lead the Church into the Third Age was claimed in the following centuries first by the Franciscans, then by Dominicans, Augustinians, and even by the Jesuits. The Holy Roman Empire itself, begun in 800 by Charlemagne, did not in fact end until 1806, with Napoleon's victory at Jena. The night before that battle, Hegel completed his *Phenomenology of Mind* which ends, appropriately, with a scheme reminiscent of Joachim of Fiori's announcement of a New Age of the Spirit to complete the Ages of the Father and the Son.

At the end of the fifteenth century Columbus proclaimed America the land of the millennium. He insisted to Ferdinand and Isabella that he had mapped his voyage in Isaiah 11:10–12. The cartographer Amerigo Vespucci, writing to Lorenzo de Medici, speaks of America (or what would later be so named in his honor) as a "New World." It was only natural that the explorers who set out to claim the new territories for the crown would be accompanied by Christian missionaries to conquer the heart of its peoples for Catholicism.

In the early seventeenth century, Protestant scholars tried to return to the faith of the first Christians and their belief that Christ would come not to end time but to bring about the golden age and the millennium. With the advance of the European Enlightenment, this came to be identified with belief in progress.

In the 1960s in the United States, at the height of a movement of religious awareness, millennialism found its way into serious theology with the death-of-God theology of Thomas Altizer, who picked up on Hegel's idea of the dawning of a new age of "self-consciousness of Spirit," and has carried this theme consistently through his writings to this day. And today, of course, millennial cults and prophecies are already tripping over one another for the attention of the religiously gullible, and we can expect more of the same in the years to come.

In literal terms, these movements and interpretations have all proved wrong. But at the same time, they show a certain sensitivity to the fact that changes—even sea changes—do take place, and are mirrored in religious fanaticism as well as, if not better than, anywhere else. Thus while there will no doubt be a great deal of nonsense to repudiate in the years to come, this does not mean that we must simply dispense with the idea that Christianity is at the dawn of a new age.

Christianity at the dawn of a new age

In a gesture that seems to run counter to what is going on in the Catholic Church at large, the Vatican has already announced preparations to celebrate the two-thousandth birthday of Christianity. The highest echelons of Catholic leadership have fallen badly out of touch with the spirit of the age, which it condemns as secular and misguided, with the result that those who breathe that spirit most energetically have come to think of the Catholic tradition as too narrow a receptacle for the religious consciousness of today. I will consider this in more detail later, but first I would like to take a quick rush through the two thousand years of Christian history in order to clarify what I see as the emergence of a new stage in that story.

1. The Teachings of Jesus

The first stage, obviously, was that of *Jesus' teaching*. Though we may never come to a clear picture of precisely what constitutes Jesus' own contribution and how much was added later, there is a substantial agreement on the main teachings, and also on the fact that, later interpretations and developments aside, there is something of universal appeal in those teachings. Even the iconoclast Nietzsche maintained enough sympathy towards Jesus to proclaim that "there was only one Christian—and he died on the cross!"[2]

To be sure, it was only after Jesus' death that his teachings were institutionalized, and hence altered to justify that institutionalization. Nietzsche's point was not merely to draw a distinction between Christ and Christianity in order to pass judgment on the latter, but also to stress the fact that the teachings of Jesus that have come down to us were worked over by the evangelists and are thus forever lost to us in their original form. No doubt a variety of motivations in the early Church contributed to the way Jesus and his ideas were remembered. But if there is no Jesus without the Christian community, neither is there any Christian community without Jesus. During the next formative period of Christianity, this mutuality was to be overshadowed by other concerns.

2. Christianism

The second stage, *Christianism* (a word that rings unfamiliar in English but is still used in modern romance languages to indicate "Christianity" in general), is marked by the transformation of the teachings of Christ into a systematization of doctrines, practices, and structures. The coordination of the teachings into a more or less consistent body of doctrines, which began already in the first generation after the death of Jesus, was marked by an immense variety of opinion and very little uniformity. As the findings of the scrolls of Nag Hammadi have continued to show us, hardly any of the major traits that have separated the Christian churches and sects from one another in later history are not represented there.

Indeed, a fair portion of the ideas that were later to be condemned as heresy were also present there.

What is more, this pluriformity spread beyond the teachings to include patterns for organization of the Christian communities. Some early leaders, like James the brother of Jesus, wanted to set religious leadership up along family lines. Even after his execution, this family principle remained around for a time, as witnessed in Jewish-Christian refugee churches after the fall of Jerusalem in 70 CE which were led by cousins of Jesus. More important, as it happened, was the idea of the primacy of Peter, based on the fact that he was the first witness of the Resurrection. In line with this mode, the three major apostles—Peter, James, and John—were all thought of as holding leading positions in the community, with the other Apostles following in importance. The churches of the Diaspora outside of Palestine showed similar variety of structure. Some followed the Jewish synagogue principle of leadership through elders. Others had charismatic or spiritually influential figures and prophets as leaders. Still others had leaders elected by the congregation. In the midst of this great variety, the one unifying element, for both doctrine and organization, was the image of the resurrected Lord which brought the two together in a basic teaching. The whole community was envisaged as a single "body" that neither local differences nor the death of any particular individuals could break up. This was symbolized in the key ritual of the Eucharistic meal.

But uniformity in structure and doctrine gradually came into force, marking the culmination of this second stage with the birth of what we now know as the hierarchical Church. This development was stimulated not only in reaction to the persecution of the Christian communities by the Roman authorities, but also by dissent in matters of organization and doctrine within the communities. Organizationally, Christianity settled on a hierarchical structure in the course of the second century. The Bishops led the worship services and administered the wealth of the churches. Doctrinally, disagreement with the Gnostic Christians served to solidify official doctrine and to eliminate potentially disruptive nonconformity. In fact, this was done so effectively that virtually all we knew about the Gnostics until recently was by way of resume appearing in Christian attacks against them.

In any case, the clarification of doctrine and organization meant not only that tradition had been established, but that the pieces were in place for another major transition, a transition that would seal the fate of pluriformity in doctrine and structure for a thousand years.

3. Christendom

The third stage, that of *Christendom*, shows the emergence of Christianity as a mode of civilization associated with the assumption of secular power. It is marked by two watershed events.

The first watershed was the conversion of Constantine the Great to Christianity in the early fourth century. (He was formally baptized, however, only shortly before his death.) In 313 Constantine proclaimed tolerance for the Christians and thereafter worked actively to transform the Roman empire into a Christian state, thus preparing the way for a distinctively Christian Western and Byzantine medieval culture. The result was that the Church was set within the boundaries of the Roman Empire, and that Christian apocalyptic expectations all but disappeared. Christendom, triumphant against persecution, now aligned itself with secular powers to become an earthly institution committed to maintain order in society.

The second watershed event is the crowning of Charlemagne, King of the Franks, as Roman Emperor by Pope Leo iii in 800. (He had already been crowned King of the Franks at age twelve by Pope Zacharias, thus settling a political dispute.) By the fifth century, the title of Roman Emperor had lapsed, but with its reinstatement the secular power of Christendom was sealed for the remainder of the middle ages. Modern historians speak of this as the "Holy Roman Empire" (a term that actually dates only from the mid-thirteenth century, though was never officially used), which lasted for fully a thousand years.

The transition to Christendom was a major shift for Christianity. In place of a multiformity of Church structures, a uniform episcopal constitution anchored in imperial law took over. In place of a diversity of creeds, a uniform, imperial confession of faith (the Nicene Creed, still read today, which was settled at a council convened in 325 by Constantine) was enforced as legally valid for all churches of the empire. In fact, it was in the early fourth century that the word "orthodoxy" was introduced by the Greek fathers. A uniform, officially sanctioned liturgy replaced former diversity. Monasticism was also standardized.

This new uniformity was not created out of nothing; it was built on the rubble of an earlier and very different idea of Christian unity. The imperially unified Church came to be delineated by the territorial boundaries of the Roman Empire. Every deviation from orthodoxy (which was fixed at imperial synods) was considered a deviation from public order. Not surprisingly, missionary activity outside of imperial territories, first among Christians living in Asian lands, met with national and political opposition among those who identified the Church as a Roman imperial institution.

In the ninth century, with the Carolingian Empire, the process was repeated within the Germanic-Roman areas. In the monastic sphere, Italian Benedictine forms defeated the pluriformity that had existed in Celtic-Scotch-Irish origins and those of Asia Minor origins. A uniform Roman liturgy replaced the multiformity of the French, Spanish, and Ambrosian liturgies, all enforced by imperial councils. The use of the Latin language was enforced from the third century (a custom that was rescinded in Catholicism only in 1962). Political guarantees for the unity of Christendom were carried out by Spanish, Portuguese, and French missionaries during the conquest of the Americas in the sixteenth century.

Neither the Orthodox schism of the eleventh century nor the Protestant reformation of the sixteenth century did much to alter this pattern. While these revolutions may have contributed to the weakening of the secular power of Roman Catholicism, they did not make any attempt to break with the ideal of Christendom or to forego all secular power for themselves, such as they had at the respective periods of their breaks from Rome.

4. Christian religion

The fourth stage belongs to our more recent past and marks the transition away from Christendom and towards seeing *Christianity as a religion,* as one religion in a multireligious world. If we were to single out a pivotal event for this turn, it would have to be the appearance of Darwin's *Origins of the Species* in 1859. In the wake of its publication, which challenged with all the authority of scientific rigor the idea of world created out of nothing by divine edict and the direct creation of human beings in an already completed world, Western intellectuals took to looking at the evolution of everything from human consciousness to social structures. The "human" sciences of religion, anthropology, sociology, and psychology all grew up at this time. In this tempest of ideas, Christianity could no longer be seen as a single, superior, divinely instituted religion, but only as one among many, and in great part a cultural phenomenon that grew and evolved out of history.

Although the Holy Roman Empire, and with it the age of Christendom, came to an end with Napoleon, Christianity's commitment to institutional strength did not. Deprived of much of its secular power, the Roman Catholic Church was not ready simply to let go of the self-understanding that had grown up in the previous millennium. Nor has it ever been ready to do so. Its achievements during this time were, of course, immensely important to Western history in particular and to the shape of world history in general, and it was on this basis that elements of Christendom have survived down to our own day.

This does not mean that Christianity was merely a passive victim, stripped against its will of a former glory. Positive steps to rethink its new role were taken in the first great wave of activity in the nineteenth century thorough a new missionary movement, first among the Protestants and then among the Catholics. In place of the sword of the conquers of the New World, culture became the nineteenth-century weapon of choice. The sewing machine in India and the bicycle in China were introductions of the missionaries who saw them as useful cathechetical aids. Convinced of the superiority of their culture and science, missionaries set out to colonize the world for the Christian religion, transplanting to the countries of Africa and Asia Western Church structures and philosophic assumptions that remain to this day.

Christianity's self-understanding as a world religion followed the pattern of the West's understanding of itself as a world culture. It remained forever *the* religion, before which all others were false or at best incomplete. The rights of truth over falsehood had of course shifted from what they had been in the past. During the renaissance, Catholics who opposed the "divine right" of pontifical states were excommunicated. And back in the middle ages those who denied the right to torture heretics were also accused of heresy. No Catholic in the nineteenth century felt obliged by these laws and injunctions of Christendom, of course. But they did feel obliged to support the internal structures that remained as definitive for Christian religion—from papal nuncios to canon law to encyclicals and ecumenical councils.

Both within Catholicism and across the spectrum of Christianity as a whole, the consequences of this shift from Christendom to Christianity as a religion are still rippling in the Christian pond. Even so, there is sufficient consensus among Christian believers throughout the world to suggest that the pieces are in place for another major change, namely, a massive turn away from the vestiges of Christendom that linger in the self-understanding of Christianity as a religion. For the better part of this century, the critique of the Danish philosopher Soren Kierkegaard against the lingering vestiges of "Christendom" in Christian religious consciousness have rung true and inspired theologians, poets, dramatists, and philosophers of all stripes to hasten the coming. Not surprisingly, keepers of the structures of Christendom have remained intransigent in clinging to what can only be a lost cause. The signs are too many and too widespread to deny that a fourth stage of Christianity is already upon us.

5. Christianness

The final stage, an era whose dawn, as I said, has already come, we might call with the Catalan philosopher of religion Raimon Panikkar, Christianness. By this he means a personal form of religious consciousness that identifies itself as Christian without belonging to a particular ecclesiastical institution. There are two modes to Christianness, both essential for this stage to have its full meaning.

The first mode is internal to Christianity. In an earlier age one could hardly call oneself Christian without belonging to Christendom. With the European enlightenment, this identification began to be eroded, and this process of disassociation continued through the rise of science, technology, communications, and travel, until today more and more Christians are open to seeing themselves as Christian in view of some sort of "Christianness" rather than of any particular affiliation. This does not entail that Christianity be simply privatized as a matter for the individual alone. I am speaking in this first case of identifying oneself with the community of the Christian heritage in a self-critical way, confessing belief in the teachings of Jesus without extending that belief to the current forms of the Christian establishment.

Whatever the intentions of the individuals who assume such a belief, its spread neither requires nor encourages the abolition of Christian institutions altogether. The defining trait of disestablished Christianity is merely a distancing of oneself from interest in the preservation or reform of the institutional Church, or at least from identifying it as the primary meaning of "Church." My perception is that belonging to Christendom, whether in its conservative or reformist branches, is not an issue for the majority of Christian believers today. This does not imply a lack of concern with the political or social order, though there are forms of this Christianness that do so neglect it. Nor does it imply that the existing institution is beyond preservation and reform. It simply means that for the first time since the first century of Christianism, disestablished faith is no longer considered by great numbers of Christians an impediment to considering oneself fully Christian. Tradition retains its importance, but only selectively. Or more precisely, the principles of selection, which are always part of the preservation of tradition, are being viewed differently.

On the positive side, this internal mode of confession of Christian faith as a personal choice means adopting a Christ-consciousness in which Christ is the central symbol of one's life. This, too, is part of the sociological fact that the Church is no longer one with ecclesiastical institutions. But it is more than a fact; it is a deed in the making. And this deed is more than the polishing of private consciousness. It also shows up in Latin America and to some extent in countries like the Philippines in the building of alternative "grass-roots" communities not only to relocate institutional affiliation, but to save spirituality from the dangerous preoccupation with self which liberation theology has struggled to point out. Once again, the relationship between the new stage and the former stage is one of criticism, not of total erasure.

Panikkar puts the shift to Christianness this way:

There is undoubtedly in the world today a certain crisis of Christian identity. Although there are revivalist movements going back to the ideal of a modernized Christendom and other more theological tendencies striving for a reformed Christianity [i.e, as a religion], there is a growing number of responsible persons who struggle to articulate a genuine Christian confession without being totally conditioned by the historical burden of the past and by the doctrinal strictures of tradition. They do not sponsor a privatization of Christian identity, although sometimes they are almost forced to it. They sponsor an exteriorization of their Christian identity that is the fruit more of inner experience than of historical and doctrinal intertias. More or less consciously aware that the world is undergoing a mutation, they are attempting to live this change at its deepest—that is, at the religious level of their consciousness and consciences. In simpler terms, a substantial number of contemporary Christians want to be religious, believers, and even Christians—but without the "contaminations" that they feel have been attached to those names.[3]

Christianness, however, is not something restricted to the consciousness of those who see Christ as their primary symbol of meaning for life. There is a second and no less important mode of Christianness, one which takes the Christian religion not only beyond the walls of ecclesiastical institutions, but beyond the frontiers of the primacy of Christ. For the turn from Christianity as a religion to Christianness also opens the possibility of those in other religions converting to Christianity without forsaking their own primary symbols or even their institutional affiliation. Conversely, it opens the possibility of Christians inheriting the religious riches of other religions, such as Buddhism and Islam, not as mere ideas, but into their own religious consciousness and practice. In short, the transition to Christianness does not do away with the Christian mission but alters its nature from a confrontation between religions to a synthesis within personal religious consciousness.

A CLASH OF VISIONS

It is premature to define this Christianness. What we can do is point to the contradictions and confrontations that accompany its birth, like the play of light and darkness meeting each other at dawn, in order to see more clearly and decide on our own participation. For I believe it is not, in the end, merely something Christianity engages in, but something that Christianity is being swept up in—namely the birth of a new vision of reality within a tired and suffocating global civilization. I will single out a number of problems characteristic of present-day Christianity, in particular Catholicism, in which we can see Christianness taking shape. I will define these problems in terms of an antagonism of opposites.

Put in the most general of terms, I see two fundamental orientations at work within Christianity today, facing individual believers with a choice. It is not a dead choice about interpreting something from the past; it is a problem that has taken hold of us *in our belief*. In the measure in which we consider ourselves Christian, we are compelled towards it. It is, moreover, a momentous choice, one that affects the meaning of life and the role of religion in it. For Christians, this live, forced, momentous option has to do with how we face the coming millennium.

As I mentioned at the outset, the third millennium wears an aura of mystique that is enhanced by the great changes going on in religious consciousness in our own day. Within Christian religion—that is to say, the realm out of which I believe Christianness is coming to birth—one finds people orienting themselves to this change in quite different ways. At one extreme are those who walk into the future backwards, and at the other, those who walk into the future head on. Although I shall align my sympathies here with the emergence of Christianness and its vision towards the future, I do not mean to identify entirely with either of the opposing positions I am about to distinguish. I set them up as extremes only to draw a spectrum along which one can identify one's own position. In the end, it is a question of orientation, not of a fixed stance.

By walking backwards, I mean facing the future with one's sight riveted on the past. One wants always to have the security of knowing where one has come from and of never losing sight of what has been accomplished in the past. New experiences are "backed into" with the models, assumptions, and expectations that one is already familiar with. The important values of history lie *behind* us, in what *has been*. This is hardly an attitude peculiar to stubborn, dogmatic religious institutions. The history of civilization's appropriation of tools, as Marshall MacLuhan pointed out so effectively a generation and more ago, shows us something similar. Technological innovations are met with habits of the technology they replace. In the sphere of religion, new adventures of the spirit are being measured by the yardstick of existing institutions, which only accents the differences and blinds one to the possibility of something radically new happening to the way Christianity establishes itself in human society.

By walking head on into the future, in contrast, I mean not being detained by the past, and indeed preferring to break with as much of it as necessary in order to create something new. The important values of history lie *ahead* of us, in what *will be*. Insofar as this attitude is embraced unconsciously, the danger of traditional models surviving in new dress is of course present. But insofar as the future is novel in a comprehensive sense, sooner or later it will have to find some way to embrace the past.

In either case, more and more Christian believers find themselves faced with this choice of orientation at the end of the century. The poles have never been so far apart; the numbers huddling in between have never been so numerous. The nature of the choice precludes a legislated response. In the end, it is up to each individual to invest feelings, imagination, and energies into the orientation of belief. The phenomena I am about to explain may be clearest in Europe and the Americas, where the confidence to stand up to the establishment in all its forms is inbred in the establishment itself, but there are signs that this mood is coming to expression throughout the Christian world, including its outer reaches in Japan.

Religious experience: New-Age spiritualities vs. institutions

As noted above, the mistrust of institutions is at an all-time high within Catholic Christianity. There are many signs of this, including the familiar rebellion against structures and attempts at overturning them. But there is a new index which is still more threatening to the institution and foreboding of a change in Catholicism itself: indifference. This is not an indifference that extends to religion in general, however, in that energies once devoted to the establishment are being deliberately rechanneled into a concern with personal religious experience.

Throughout its history, Christianity has nourished, deliberately, a distrust of religious experience. The *contemplatio* of the middle ages which encouraged discovery of God within and union with the divine led to opinions that often incurred condemnation and excommunication. Later ages, which saw the need to recognize what is of value in this tendency and yet to keep it at arm's length from mainstream Christianity, came to speak of it as "mysticism." The same Eckhart whose writings were condemned in his own lifetime—and to this day his condemnation has not been repealed by the Vatican—has become a hero of modern spirituality. Moreover, one sees a rediscovery of interest in the "love mysticism" of Hadewijch and Jan van Ruusbroec, as well as in the esoteric tradition that includes everything from witchcraft to alchemy, Christian and otherwise. In all of this, one sees a longing for direct religious experience, and by implication for direct contact with a Reality that has been imprisoned behind the iron bars of sacred texts and official doctrine.

There is much to applaud in such longing; but there is also something distressing about the so-called "new age spirituality" in Christianity (my impression is that it is strongest among those from the Catholic background) and about the industry that has arisen to feed on it. The interest in direct-access religious experience aimed at self-discovery and self-fulfillment is no doubt an index of frustration with the intransigence and reactionary attitude of the organized churches. But it is also a sign of an epidemic of spiritual immaturity that afflicts our times. For one thing, the stress on personalism focuses on improving the quality of life of individuals, not of communities. Their optimism of "empowerment" and "transformation" is more a resignation to structural social evils than a real resistance. Taichi, art therapy, enneagrams, spiritual journals, Feldenkreis movement, psychosynthesis, body therapy, eco-spiritualities, and the like often commonly involve a rejection of institutional boundaries and standards that includes both religion and science. As that keen observer of Catholic spirituality Eugene Kennedy has remarked, "this intense activity could not exist without the institutional Catholicism from whose groaning structures they provide seasonal escape…. This is nothing but MacSpirituality, junk food for the soul…. It is Disneyland posing as Chartres."[4]

Obviously, this is not the whole picture of spirituality, but it is among the strongest energies in Catholicism today. The spiritual classics of the West are gathering dust while populraist manuals offering to "change your life" are taking their place for more and more people, including a sizable number of clergy and religious.

If religious maturity is not guaranteed by strong, impregnable institutions, neither is it the fruit of preoccupation with self-fulfillment. It is finally not about finding the self and enhancing its qualities but about seeing through the self and losing it. Nevertheless, it seems to me that the longing for direct religious experience does serve to heighten the atmosphere in which Christianness is coming to birth. Neither self-centered spiritualities nor institutional intransigence do justice to the spirit of our times; they are both, ultimately, alternative ways of dropping out. Perhaps this is why the antagonism between the two positions rarely erupts into open confrontation. It is an antagonism of indifference. While the one continues to look to the past, the other looks to itself; neither of them bothers much about the future. The coming age of Christianness demands a revolution in spirituality, a maturing beyond these first steps to a vision that looks ahead and outside of the seer. I use the word "maturity" deliberately, because I continue to believe that it is out of the spiritual energies being dissipated on self-preoccupation that such a new spirituality will arise. This maturity is being prompted by other concerns, a number of which we will take up next.

Interreligiosity: Fundamentalism vs. dialogue

The Dalai Lama remarked in a session I attended last summer that "today and in the near future, there are two alternatives: fundamentalism or interreligious dialogue." This is, to the best of my knowledge, the first time in history that a religious figure of his stature has made such a statement. While it may not represent the view of the masses of Buddhist believers, let alone of Tibetan Buddhists, it does, I believe, point to interreligiosity as an important ingredient in the spirituality that lies ahead for us.

The contrasting attitudes to other religions signalled by the terms "fundamentalism" and "interreligious dialogue" is very much alive in Christianity. There is a whole range of meanings carried by the term "fundamentalism," but in the Christian context I take it to mean basically the following: that the Christian tradition has in its possession texts that constitute the truth of God's salvific plan for all of creation and its sole complete source of reference; that these texts are without error and cannot be contradicted by discoveries of science or human experience of any kind; and that no other religion can lead to truth or salvation except it succumb to belief in these texts. In essentials, it is committed to walking backwards into all futures, including our own.

Dialogue, on the other hand, begins from a commitment to the plurality of religious ways and the development of religious truth. It does not imply a relativism of all religious ways—clearly some are better than others or wiser than others—nor does it deny the right of a body of religious truth to claim absoluteness for itself. What it does say is simply that all religious ways are "on the way," developing, imperfect grasps of their own truth, and that hence a plurality of absolute religious claims need not end in a battle for conversion of each other's members, but can lead to the ongoing maturity of each. It walks forward into the future not only because of a temperament that disposes it to do so, but because there is nowhere in the past to look for a road. In many matters, in fact, it *must* turn its back on the past in order to prepare for what lies ahead.

This does not mean that an interreligious spirituality abandons the goal of converting the world to Christ. The idea of converting the world to Christendom or to the Christian religion may be an anachronism, but the hope of converting the world to Christianness is not. If dialogue takes place only at the level of turning theology towards the history of religions, of criticizing the narrow-minded, closed attitude of an earlier age, then it has not gotten beyond the vestibule of its responsibilities. The sacred task is that of mutual conversion, and this is a river in which current interreligious efforts have hardly gotten their feet wet. The world has now become mission territory for all religions, but we must not allow this to become like a market economy where some establishments reinforce themselves through the weakening of others. There are no "losers" in an interreligious world. But until we can redefine "winning," the work of building such a world in earnest cannot begin.

The clash of visions between fundamentalism and dialogue is not something restricted to the circle of Church theologians. It is a matter of importance for the masses of Christianity, and the gains go far beyond intellectual advance. And it is out of this clash that the Christianity of the future is taking shape.

Knowledge: Doctrine vs. science

A third clash of visions within Christianity today has to do with the battle between doctrine and science for "true knowledge." This is a battle that has been with us since the rise of modern science, but it has become a popular problem for ordinary believers only in the twentieth century with the spread of scientific education and dependence on science in the workplace. On this issue Christianity is clearly divided, and this is a division that really goes to the heart of Western culture today. The technological civilization we live in is based on science, but when it comes to matters of religion we still prefer to turn away from science into traditional theological formulations.

Walking into the scientific future with one's eyes on the religious doctrine of the past is, of course, a direct extension of religious fundamentalism. It views the revelations of the bible—and in the case of Catholicism, the pronouncements of Church tradition also—as a standard for the advance of secular knowledge. But this is its weakest form. More dangerous still, and also more popular, is the view that after all religion does not have to do with the same subject matter as science. The world of "transhistorical" truth and "religious realities" transcend the advances of science and can never be challenged by it because science cannot have the tools to evaluate it. In both cases, religious knowledge keeps its gaze fixed on the past as the source of value and marches backwards into the future of Christianity. The problem is that when it comes to concrete moral judgments, the testing ground for all truth, the individual believer is left at a loss. Abstract doctrines floating in the air on the one hand, concrete facts weighing us down with their inevitability on the other.

But the schizophrenia cries out for a cure. One cannot depend on scientific knowledge for a livelihood, and then simply set it aside when it comes to matters of religion. The desire to escape this conundrum has given rise to comprehensive, "cosmic" visions of the most preposterous sorts that claim to accept all of science and justify all of religion. They do so, of course, only by keeping clear of the rigors of both in order to create a kind of fairy-tale world that intellectual conscience cannot touch. The reasons for the success of such schemes are not entirely on the side of the new visionaries. Throughout this century, as science made inroads into traditional revealed truths, Christian churches of all stripes have taken a predominantly reactionary stance towards the scientific community. The reaction against evolutionary theory is still going on in parts of the Christian fundamentalist world. And in the Catholic world, no less a brilliant science and religious thinker as Teilhard de Chardin was banished and his most important work condemned to be published only after his death. Today his thought is still a living inspiration for those who prefer to march forward into the future of Christianity. But even though his ideas have become part of theological training in Catholic seminaries across the world, official Church theology has yet to catch up with the scientific revolution of the seventeenth century, much less with the still greater advances of our own age.

The more important result one expects from the clash is that somehow the teaching and person of Christ will guide our accumulating and use of knowledge, whatever its source, towards the good of all that lives. This requires a metanoia which, I believe, is another key ingredient in the advance towards Christianness. I cite Teilhard's words here, forbidden publication in the 1930's when they were written:

> Our generation and the two that preceded it have heard little but talk of the conflict between science and faith; indeed it seemed at one moment a foregone conclusion that the former was destined to

take the place of the latter.... After close on two centuries of passionate struggles, neither science nor faith has succeeded in discrediting its adversary. On the contrary, it becomes obvious that neither can develop normally without the other. And the reason is simple: the same life animates both.... For we are not human beings having a spiritual experience. We are spiritual beings having a human experience.[5]

Such a metanoia sees that the primary scripture is life in all its forms, that the bible, the Buddhist canon, the Koran on the one hand, and the deliverances of science on the other, are chapters of it. Christianity must never forget its obligation to convert science, but that conversion is not to a doctrine that sets up certain *facts* around which science has to work. The conversion must rather be to Christianness, which does not represent a rock-solid "base" judging what is true knowledge and what is not, but a kind of "dome," an uplifting that turns the eyes of the working scientist away from the matter at hand and towards the greater context of life.

Culture: Particularity vs. uniformity

Finally, I would point to a clash of visions between those who see the universality of Christianity as the dominion of certain determined patterns, and those who see universalizing as a sacralization of the specific. Culture has become a weapon from which Christianity must learn to disarm itself. The churches of Asia, Africa, and Micronesia continue to set themselves up according to structures inherited from the West, and to train sacred ministers according to a class structure not only several centuries out of date but from a history that has never been their own. The only explanation for the survival of such habits of thought is an unchallenged conviction of cultural superiority—be it conscious or unconscious—that is shared in by Christian leaders both in the West and outside of it.

This clash has produced so little in the way of concrete change from the central churches, as witnessed in the intransigence of the

Vatican, that we find a generation of Christians growing up eager to take Christianity into their own hands and their own culture. In most cases, this leads to a breaking away from the official churches. If I am right and the spirituality of Christianness continues to take hold of more and more of the minds and hearts of Christians across the world, I suspect we will see more breakaway churches in the years to come. In the context of the clash between pluriformity and uniformity, this is almost inevitable.

Meantime, within the official churches the most forward-looking voices among the colonized Christians are still voices that rattle the chains of their captivity. Positive, creative responses are all too few. There are many, on the other hand, who see the "universality" of the Church as a way of protecting the Church from being swallowed up by the local culture, as for instance Protestantism was by Japanese militarism during the past war. But the fact that this "universalizing" is indelibly Western seems no more than a mild annoyance; indeed the otherness is welcomed, with the result that the impact on local cultures is minimized. In their case, walking backwards into the future means keeping one's eyes on the West, the countries from which Christianity first arrived. Walking forwards means taking Christianity where it has not yet gone—into the soul of culture of another religious background.

CONCLUSION

The conflicts I have pointed to above are very real, and the usual way of drawing the antagonisms—evangelicals and fundamentalists on the one side and liberal theologians on the other; Vatican curia on the one side, grass-roots communities on the other—is not mere fiction. Still, it has been my aim to cut across these usual divisions in order to suggest a clash of visions between those obedient (*ob-audire*) to the age, and those deaf to it.

Why should we listen to the age? Is it not all wrong, after all? Does religion not always have to stand against the saeculum now that our experiment with Christendom has been proven a disaster?

The saeculum is never purely secular but always has its religious side—a kind of secular religiosity—and therefore prompts another set of questions in reply to the religious critique of secularism. Do not all religions believe in a kind of higher inspiration that transcends structures, individuals, and reason? Do they not organize themselves around the belief that their very survival depends on something outside of themselves? Then why is it that those who step aside from conventional religious doctrine and structures should be de facto cut off from access to that inspiration? It is the height of religious disbelief to refuse in principle to seek out the positive *yearning* behind the obvious secularism of the age, a yearning not addressed by conventional religion.

I remember many years ago being called into the office of the president of Nanzan University, Johannes Hirschmeier, to consult on some matter or other. After completing our business we sat down for a cup of tea. At one point he opened his wallet and read out the following passage to me:

> Fathers grow accustomed to descend to the level of their sons and fear them, and the son is on a level with his father, having no respect or reverence for either of his parents. And this is his freedom. And foreign residents are equal with ordinary citizens and citizens with foreign residents, and visiting foreigners are as good as either of them.... Teachers fear and flatter their students, and students despise their teachers and tutors; there is no distinction between old and young; the young man is on a level with the old and is ready to compete with him in word or deed; and old men condescend to the young and are full of pleasantry and gaiety; fearing to become morose and authoritative, they adopt the manners of the young.... And of course we cannot forget to mention the liberty and equality of the sexes in relation to each other.[6]

He asked what I thought of it and I remarked that I was rather astonished to find a university president, whose influence weighs heavily on the young people entrusted to his care, carrying something so negative around with him. He laughed and told me I ought to know better. The passage had been photocopied from a page of Plato's *Republic,* and he kept it wherever he went in order to remind himself that so many of the problems advertised to us as new and unique to our time or our culture—and which we devote so much effort and thought to—are as old as human society itself. It is not that this makes them less real, but rather that they must not be allowed to derail our consciences into thinking we have grasped the fundamental spirit of our age when we have only spent ourselves on the peripherals. Although our opinions differed on a great many things, the surprise was sobering. To this day, when I meet a university president, I cannot help but wonder if the only things he carries around in his wallet is his credit cards and money.

I believe the Dalai Lama is right about the need to choose between fundamentalism and dialogue, but I also believe that, in the Christian world and perhaps in the Buddhist as well, this choice belongs to something greater that is happening to our age—something that inspires sensitive spiritual leaders to say such things, something that nudges closed institutions of good will, almost against their will, to open up. And that something, that "spirit" must be named holy as we step into the next century. Otherwise, I see no way that we can face the great moral challenges posed to us by the megalopolis, the globalization of poverty, the dwindling protection of human rights, and the trashing of as much of the cosmos as our civilization can get its hands on. These are not in themselves religious problem, but they *are* problems for religion. Their appearance must not be used to justify turning us away from our age and back to old modes of thought. They are rather the final test of how holy our spirit will turn out to be.

NOTES

[1] Most recently a book entitled *The Choice: Islam and Christianity* by a certain Ahmed Deedat came into my hands. Privately published in the Republic of South Africa in 1993, it is already in its sixteenth printing and has run to 223,000 copies.

Its opening pages identify the pope of Rome as the beast of the Apocalypse, setting the tone for the rest of the volume.

[2] *The Antichrist*, sec. 39.

[3] Raimon Panikkar, "Christianity and Christianness." Kuncheria Pathil, ed., *Church in the Third Millennium, Jeevadhara* 21 (1991): 324–30. As it turns out, Panikkar's "neologism" is not so new. In the passage cited in the previous note, Nietzsche makes mention of "Christlichkeit."

[4] "New Age Spirituality," *Notre Dame Magazine* (Spring 1992): 22–3.

[5] *The Phenomenon of Man* (New York: Harper Torchbooks, 1959), 283ff.

[6] Plato, The Republic IV [14], 562–3.

What Time Is It
for Christianity?

In the late summer of 1997 a group of twenty-five missiolo-gists from Asia was gathered in Nagoya for a week-long conference on the challenge of millennial movements for the Churches. I was asked to prepare the keynote address for the occasion.

Reading through what literature I could get my hands on, I was struck by the coincidental timing of the arrival of millennial movements on the scene and the remission of established Christianity. In my address I tried to suggest that to see the coincidence as graced—that is, as a kairos— requires a renunciation of the effort to keep pace with events and to find an answer for every challenge. In that vein, I took the question, "What time is it for Christianity?" not as a question about what the institutions identified with Chris-tianity are supposed to be doing at this point in their story, but what the larger story of our times, whether through cun-ning providence or the mere mindless flow of events, seems to be doing with Christianity.

Published simultaneously in *Metanoia* 8:3/4 (1998): 99-121 and, in Czechoslovakian translation, in *Cĕská Metanoia* 18 (1998): 11-32.

IT IS SAFE TO PREDICT that the end of the millennium will see an extravagance of new religious movements proclaiming the impending end of the world as we know it, the final confrontation between the forces of Good and Evil, the collapse of modern civilization, the dawn of a new age, and similar apocalyptic phenomena. It is equally safe to predict that the Church will face these movements more or less uniformly with the following kinds of questions:

- Why do people allow themselves to be deceived by such movements whose prophecies inevitably end up unfulfilled? What possible need can they be filling?
- What can the Church do to safeguard its faithful from falling prey to this kind of deception?
- What can be done to revive the Church's own eschatological doctrine and present it anew as a believable alternative?
- With our new technologies and communications, can we expect to see any movements of a global nature that will require the Church to join forces with those of other religions in the effort to stop the wider human community from further harming itself?

Whatever the answers, it is unlikely that any reasonable, studied measures the religious establishments of the world take will do very much to cool the millennial fever. This, too, is predictable: the unknown and uncontrollable forces in the human spirit that greet turning points in history with religious fanaticism are not about to let themselves be easily corralled into the secular forum of religious academia or into the sacred spaces of organized religion. Something momentous is in store for the world of religion and there seems to be very little we can do to prepare for it.

The theological enlightenment of the last fifty years has penetrated too deeply into the ecclesial establishment to expect the Church to participate in the mystique of the end of the millennium other than in a tame and civil manner. Biblical studies have advanced too far to expect a return to a former fascination with historical prophecies tied to specific dates and numbers. Surely nothing like the apocalyptic commotion surrounding the turn to the eleventh century will shake the Church's turn to the twenty-first, dividing religious orders and local churches against one another and against the central authorities. There is some comfort in this, but at a price: the Church is at a distinct psychological disadvantage when it comes to asserting its own authority in the face of cults and movements that feed on the residual superstitions and enchanted hopes of the masses of believers who have not kept pace with religious scholarship. At the level of religious sentiment, it is a battle Christianity cannot win.

The predicament that the advent of the third millennium poses for the Church is not merely one of reasonable faith pitted against the darkness of superstition. It is symbolic of a shift taking place within Christian consciousness itself. Every step the Church takes towards or away from the modern world seems to chip away another piece of the tain at the back of the mirror, until it can barely see its own reflection any longer in the saeculum. Nothing the Church does to accommodate itself to modernity or to confront it seems to make much of a difference. Competition within the ranks of the institution to commit its considerable resources to liberating the poor and the oppressed, to preserving an ailing environment, to shoring up traditional beliefs, morals, and piety against the black tide of paganism and unbelief—everything begins to look more and more like a temporary distraction from a change of heart coming to birth within Christian consciousness. Whether the closing of the millennial cycle and the problems it presents to the ecclesiastical establishment are merely accidental to this deeper problem or turn out to merit the name of Holy

Providence is a question for hindsight to moot. For now, it is enough to note the coincidence.

READING THE SIGNS OF CONTRADICTION

As Jan Van Bragt has noted, "The periodicization of history found in apocalyptic literature appears to correspond to a human desire to know 'what time it is in history.'"[1] In the few years remaining to the millennium, that desire is sure to come to the fore in prophetic literature of all sorts purporting to tell us, in no uncertain terms, where it is all going and when it will get there. These questions are sure to stimulate traditional religions across the world to give their own readings of the signs of the times and make efforts to find an audience to listen to them. In all of this, there is not likely to be much new in the way of rational content to the claims that the day of reckoning is approaching for capitalism, science and technology, urban culture, nation-states, Western civilization, and so forth. The critique of modernity has been around for too long, and the debate too widely covered among the intelligentsia and in the media to expect much novelty of argument.

The appeal of apocalyptic literature will depend much less on new teachings than on new ways of fixing emotional content to already familiar criticisms. The religious movements at the turn of the millennial cycle that will reach popular sentiment are those whose symbols will make a direct link between the deep-seated desire to know what time it is in history on the one hand, and the desire to get out from under the heel of the current order of things on the other. And if they are to take full advantage of the apocalyptic mood, they will also have to deaden the capacity for detached, disinterested reason and heighten the awareness of a helpless disenfranchisement from the status quo. To borrow a celebrated phrase, they will have to combine in themselves the ambivalent role that Christianity once played but can play no longer: the opium of the people, the cry of the oppressed.[2]

Indulge me the prediction that in the near future new religious movements will feed irrational, fundamentalistic doctrines to masses of people disenchanted with the way the world is going, and that this will unleash an energy that will even attract considerable numbers of the Christian faithful. Let us suppose further that even though the mainline churches as such will not be swept into apocalyptic prophecies of their own, many of its preachers will concede to the clamor for talk about demons, apparitions, revelations, and divine retributions, and in the process will seriously compromise the calm, reasoned voice of theological reflection that our century has worked so hard to cultivate. Would this not be just the time for the churches to reassert their authority boldly in an effort to save religiosity from its baser impulses?

If the present is seen primarily as the projection of a particular accumulated past into a particular immediate future, then it follows that when attacked, it is time to react. But if that structure has broken down, if the circumference has loosened and the center dispersed, as happens at great turning points in history, there is no longer a definable "inside" to ward against a menace from "outside." Insofar as the Church is no longer able to face the present as master of its own agenda, decisions about what it is time for are no longer in its own hands. The chronological model of extending a certain form of institutional presence into the future will have to give way to a kairological discernment of an uncertain future. I do not mean that the Church should at any point simply throw up its arms and cease to speak in season and out of season. But at the same time, it will have to come to terms with its own powerlessness as a historical event that cannot be blamed completely on the age's hardness of heart.

The phenomena of millennial religiosity, whatever form they take within the churches and without, are much more likely to be calmed and civilized by secular forces than by any concerted effort on the part of institutional Christianity. There is no reason to think the churches will be any more relevant to the religious movements at the end of the millennium than they are to the movements of the present day. We do not need to wait for the impending menace of new religious movements to ask what time it is for Christianity in history. The signs are all about us that the

Church is already riddled with contradictions that it is not equipped to answer, and that in its present form its time is up.

In the case of Roman Catholicism, the Vatican's intransigence on matters like curial bureaucracy, clericalism, and the devaluation of women mightily contradict the consensus fidelium of the Church at large and the published opinions of its theologians.[3] But even so, these are issues that divide the Church and not society at large, which cares very little whether that Church or any other is divided against itself or not.[4] The churches may have already graduated from the apocalyptic movements that are in store for the age, but this matters little if the age has already graduated from the churches—and that not merely from weakness of character but from what we can only call a surplus of spiritual energy. It is little wonder in such circumstances that prophetic voices in the churches speak of that energy as having been siphoned off from the communion of the faithful, where it tends to stagnate, in order to serve causes and movements that promise more direct connection with the needs of the age.

What we are talking about here is a way of perceiving Christianity very different from the way it is perceived within Christianity's dominant institutions. It is not for that reason unworthy, but neither is made more acceptable simply by being so widely accepted. To ask, from a standpoint of Christian faith, what time it is for Christianity requires both perceptions at the same time. It means looking at things with a pair of glasses whose lenses have been ground independently of each other. Through one eye we see the Christian churches as largely irrelevant; through the other, as a trustworthy deposit of the Christian story. The resulting image is a dizzy blear. Would there were some place to stand where we could remove our glasses and look at ourselves objectively, in a kind of immaculate perception free of all bias, there to ground our faith in certitude. The only sure way to stop the headache of being a Christian in the spiritual environment at the end of the twentieth century seems to be to close one eye or the other, gaining in peace of mind what one loses in depth of vision.

We must take care not to reduce the problem to a simple double-bind of competing perceptions, one Christian and one not. The signs of contradiction have coiled up within Christian consciousness itself at its most alert. The most persuasive ideas of contemporary theology, forged in concert with the critique of organized religion—interreligious dialogue, inculturation, and orthopraxis—seem to lead us not to institutional renewal but to aporia.

For a minority of the Church, albeit a minority empowered with hierarchical authority, such ideas have proved a dangerous flirtation with forces inimical to Christianity, whether because they erode faith with secular unbelief or because they expose traditional beliefs to relativity, superstition, and secularization. For a majority of Church-affiliated believers, these ideas have become part of the intellectual atmosphere in which Christianity must renew itself. In order to breathe that air freely, more and more Christians are joining the ranks of those outside organized Christianity for whom the ideological struggle with the institutional church makes little or no claim on attention. This is what I mean by saying that these ideas end in aporia: the attempt to appropriate the fruits of contemporary theological reflection casts the institution itself into doubt.

Interreligious dialogue and the retreat from doctrinal authority

Consider Christian participation in *interreligious dialogue*. At least for as long as I have been involved in formal dialogue among the religions of Asia, the stress has been on rethinking doctrine, placing it historically, recognizing the relativity of the forms in which its is expressed, including the relativity of the ways in which it lays claim to being absolute. While other forms of interreligious encounter have focused on ritual, meditation, prayer, and social action, the dialogue among scholars has been preoccupied with making sense not only to those participating but to any person into whose hands the literature should fall. Those who have come to the dialogue seeking new forms of self-understanding and new expressions for old symbols, have found themselves on a forum which demands and rewards the discipline of clear thinking. The mutual criticism and appreciation of dialogue at its best has always been driven by the desire finally to make sense. For all that, as we are reminded again and again, the dialogue has failed to make sense to the dominant institutions of the Christian faith, and has made worse sense of all to Church leaders in countries whose foundational spiritual heritage is other than Christian.

Meantime, the spirituality of the age has rushed ahead on its own. The masses of those driven by the mood of the time to lay some claim to the truth of the world's religions as their own rightful inheritance have not, by and large, subscribed to the conventions of the dialogical forum, let alone heeded the warnings and prescriptions of organized religions. A minority shifts affiliations from one world religion to another; a larger percentage simply piggy-backs a second religion to that of their upbringing[5]; most are content with a spirituality of taste-and-see that pledges allegiance to no religion in particular and does not associate immediate religious experience with religious affiliation.[6] The more discipline and effort is put by one faith tradition into taking the truths of another tradition seriously, the more it seems that new spiritualities rise up to crisscross vocabularies, concepts, and symbols without a thought to the minimal rational requirements of sustaining either tradition through time.

To the weighty expectations of academia, much of this looks bowdlerized; to those caught up in the experiment of interreligiosity, the demands of the academic dialogue seem quaint and dated. What both sides agree on in their vastly different appropriations of the encounter among religions is that they breathe easily in a religiously plural world and find the efforts of the traditional churches to assert their doctrinal authority against that world increasingly suffocating.

Inculturation and the retreat from Christian culture

The idea of *inculturation* offers a second instance of an insight whose advance in Christian consciousness is accompanied by a retreat from confidence in the role of the Church in the world. The paradigm of a universal "Christian culture," long a problem in Asia, Africa, and Latin America, has lost its persuasiveness in the West. In theological circles, the notion of inculturation has been advanced as an antidote to an exaggerated identification of Christianity with a particular cultural frame, an identification reinforced by the scientific, economic, and technological advances that have propelled the classical Christian countries of the West into a position of leadership in the world. The idea of a transcultural Christian truth attaching itself to the spread of Western civilization, however, continues to enjoy the support of the Church. To cite words recently spoken to an Asian audience by the Cardinal Prefect of the Congregation for the Doctrine of the Faith:

> It is not only the case that the convergence of mankind towards a single community with a common life and destiny is unstoppable because such an inclination is grounded in man's essence, but also because the diffusion of technological civilization is *irrevocable*.... [It] alters the interpretation of the world at its base. It changes standards and behavior. The religious cosmos is *necessarily* moved by it.... The division of Western heritage into the useful which one accepts, and the foreign, which one rejects, does not lead to the salvation of ancient cultures.[7]

This is precisely the view of the world that scholars of inculturation theory struggle against, at the same time as they are at pains to disassociate the idea from the simple transplant of one nationalism or ethnocentrism for another. But while they rummage through the scriptures and the arcana of the Christian heritage in search of ways to cope with the cultural reality of religious beliefs and practices at odds with received Christian tradition, the nonwestern churches remain interned in a kind of second-class citizenship. The "third Church" whose coming the prophets of missiology were foretelling a generation ago barely got beyond lacing its shoes before its original enthusiasm collapsed in feelings of bitter disappointment. As Raimon Panikkar puts it:

Concerned with its inner growth and self-understanding, ...Christian thought has been rather introverted. It has developed its theology within the cultural boundaries of the Western world and its colonies.... It has been said time and again, mainly from Asian sources, that Christian self-consciousness will never... apply *metanoia* to itself.[8]

Meantime, the "culture" in which Christianity is said to have taken root and flourished has been so fragmented in the modern mind that it can hardly hold its identity together without appealing to its progress in the production of goods, the marketing of services and information, and the accumulation of capital. In other words, as the critics of modernity remind us with uninterrupted regularity, when people in classical Christian cultures talk of cultural revolution, cultural enhancement, or cultural enlightenment around the world, they think primarily of "development" in those areas in which the West leads the world. Few look with any confidence to the religious past of the West for paradigms. Those who, from a position of faith, seek the preservation of cultural variety and look to the future of nonwestern forms of Christianity are systematically nudged out of the picture by an institutional Church that seems stuck in the neocolonial vocation of Christianizing a global culture.

Orthopraxis and the retreat from Christian morality

A third major idea of the age whose spread in Christian consciousness has sown the seeds of doubt about the very Christian institutions it has aimed to serve is that of *orthopraxis*. The range of this term extends from the liberation-theological reading of the scriptures to the deployment of the legions of professional associations in social action in the name of Christian principles. To complement the standards of orthodoxy, the standards of orthopraxis seek to bring into account the concrete consequences of Christian doctrine in the historical world. Unlike orthodoxy, the critique of praxis is not aimed at clarifying old teachings or denouncing new heresies in the light of scripture or tradition, but at evaluating the ritual, linguistic, symbolic, and institutional forms in which doctrine is encased for their social and environmental effects.

It was only a matter of time for the vicious circle to be drawn: the more Church authorities resisted the encroachment of social philosophy in matters of doctrine, the more intensely did the focus of the critique shift to the complicity of the Church in impersonal, institutionalized evils of the age; and the more Church authority came under fire, the more did the resistance give way to condemnation.

Meantime, the role of orthopraxis in theology battens and grows stronger through contact with the secular humanism of the day. There is no doubt that moral concern with things like the preservation of the earth and its life forms, the place of women in society, the protection of cultural and ethnic variety, and the right to good work—all of which have found their place in Christian ethics not as a result of reflection on its own sources but by listening to voices outside of organized religion—has given a new vitality to the theological enterprise. It has also heightened the sense of urgency about liberating theology from its self-serving interests. But even as all of this is going on, when it comes to the most critical moral issues of the day, the teaching authority of the official Churches, and by association of its theologians, has been edged further and further out of the picture, to the point that Christian ethics today clings to the shirttails of the saeculum for dear life.[9] The discovery and exercise of standards of orthopraxis, far from countering this tendency, has ended up heightening doubts about the ability of institutional Christianity to say anything meaningful to its faithful about morality if it is not first stamped with approval by the general humanism of the day.

The twentieth century has seen Christianity convert from a position of confrontation with the modern world to one of critical openness. The idea of the churches as oases of sanity and truth in the world but not of it, as voices of belief crying in a wilderness of unbelief, belongs to another age. Yet none of those who worked to bring about this conversion would have contemplated reaching

the point we are at today, where every step taken towards aggior-
namento seems to sink the Church deeper into anachronism,
where believers who want a worldview in which to locate their
moral concerns and the central symbols of their Christian faith
turn to spiritualities of mystical, esoteric, prechristian, even magi-
cal character. Christian faith is drifting away from the *fanum* of
the Church towards the *paganum* of the age. This I take to be a
sociological fact, open to opposing interpretations and strategies,
but a fact nonetheless. And around this fact, like planets around
the sun, revolve the contradictions whose signs are becoming
more and more evident.[10]

TELLING KAIROS

The outlook from inside the walls of organized Christianity, at
least from the standpoint outlined above, is not bright. For the
Church the road ahead to the end of the century seems fore-
doomed to be one of shadow-boxing with the saeculum in the
vain effort to identify what it is that is draining the life's blood
from ecclesiastical structures. In such circumstances, the logical
course would seem to be to issue a call for all-out internal reform,
to rally what resources it can around major inspirational ideas like
those of dialogue and inculturation and orthopraxis, hoisting
them on a higher banner, shouting them more loudly from the
pulpits, nailing them to the doors of the cathedrals. Perhaps, but
that is not the impression I meant to leave. In the spirit of this
conference on millennial movements, you will perhaps forgive me
if I tap a few more notes in the key of prediction before offering
what specific suggestions I may.

The Church is not going to reform itself.[11] Suppose it could
muster the will to do so; nothing it could achieve in the way of
redistributing existing authority and resources—the current focus
of debate—would help it cope with a turning point in history of
more radical dimensions. Even the audience of those prepared to
discuss these questions out of a sense of duty or apprehension for
the future of the Church is already too small to bear the burden of

keeping the Christian story alive in the next millennium. It will have to depend on a wider view of Christianity than an ecclesial one.[12] The high-water mark of its institutional presence around the world has been reached and its tides are receding. Perhaps it will be objected that "Church" is not primarily the institution with its ruling bureaucracy, functionaries, and hierarchical authority, but the core of the faithful; or that doctrine is not primarily the function of pronouncements from above, but of the consensus of a reflective faithful. But these are theological distinctions that pale in the face of the fact of what is happening to the mainline Churches of Christianity. Time has turned a corner for Christianity.

That having been said, the Church *will* be reformed. Kicking and screaming or limp and whining, it *is* being taken away from its past to a new and very different future. The importance of the institutional Church as representative of the deposit of Christian symbols and beliefs—by which I mean the role played by disciplined, devoted forms of institutional Christianity at both the local and international levels—cannot simply be dismissed. If anything, it will have to play a stronger role than it does now. For this to happen, the churches will need a different notion of "strength."

Current models of affiliation and organization will have to change. I doubt that this kind of change can be planned, even with the best theological reflection. It is more in the nature of a historical event to be witnessed, and then to be named not as divine retribution against a sinful humanity but as the call to a higher vocation. The exodus of faithful from the pews on the one hand, and the steady drain of attention away from theological ideas on the other, will continue at a quickened pace. Just how much Christianity will have to be bled of its ecclesial power and worldly holdings before it recovers its strength is hard to say. What seems clear to me is that a radical disestablishment has only just begun.[13]

If this is so, and the crisis that is tearing at the Church (κρινεῖν) is indeed a graced opportunity (καιρός), then the lines of division and interaction between the genius of Christianity and the genius of the age need to be redrawn. We cannot simply appeal to a model of grace pouring through the church from outer space or outer time to the world. Neither is it much help to think in terms of a spiritual hydraulics in which a given pool of native human religiosity is drained, channeled, dammed, or otherwise diverted from a common source to different destinations. Both models tilt towards a kind of elitism that puts the observer above the course of events, looking at things from the outside and deciding who has grasped what is essential to the spirit of the times and who has missed the point or been caught up in the accidentals.

The fact is, we are all caught up in the play of light and shadow. To see this time as kairos requires a spirituality of critical attention to what is going on with an eye to discerning what we ought to make be and what we ought to let be. In the classical terms of Asian wisdom, it is learning the art of a doing that is a not-doing and a not-doing that is a doing.

Christian faith turns to the archetype of a "Holy Spirit" to explain sea changes that take place for unknown and uncontrollable reasons but which we must find a way to trust. To those who do not share that sense of reliance, the belief may look like no more than blind resignation to the course of events. To know it is not to gain access to information about the world closed off to ordinary powers of reason. The ground of trust in history as providence does not lie in the *data* of the past but in the *acta* that follow from it. This is the peculiar trait of belief in a Holy Spirit: its foundations lie in the future; its justification rests on experimenting with its truth in the history that lies immediately before us. At turning points in history, like the one that faces Christianity in our own times, this experimentation is never a matter of simple determination to preserve the way things have been or simple resignation to the way things are going. Nor is it a question of drawing up blueprints for wholesale revolution of existing institutions. It is always and ever some blend of letting-be and making-be, on a scale small enough to fall within the reach of the discernment and appropriation of the individual. The art of telling kairos cannot be managed hierarchically. It is exercised at the lowest levels of social structure or it is not exercised. Against that backdrop of assumptions, I should like now to draw closer to concrete suggestions.

MODUS VIVENDI, MODUS MORIENDI

The three pivotal ideas which I singled out as signs of contradiction within the Church—dialogue, inculturation, and orthopraxis—may be bound to a theological vocabulary and logic whose influence is on the wane, even among the majority of Christians, but this is not because the insights they offer have been exhausted. In terms of institutionalized Christianity, it is not that they have been tried and found wanting but that they have not yet been tried. They point, I believe, as clearly as any ideas can point today, to the need for circumventing confrontations with church authorities and working on behalf of an alternative Christian mission. One half of that mission has to do with learning how to die gracefully to much of what our inherited mission has built up; the other, to learning how to rebuild slowly and at an appropriate scale structures suited to the conduct of Christian faith today. Let us look more closely at the kinds of decisions this living-in-dying entails.

Steps need to be taken to contain the housekeeping of Christian institutions from trampling on the spiritual sensitivities of the age.

The ethics of creating funds for the poor or maintaining organizations to serve them by investing wealth in the very structures that systematize that poverty is still very unclear. The bald moral indictment is not enough. Obviously no mission engaged in propagating the faith can survive without theological foundations it understands. It should be just as obvious that no mission can afford to erect institutions and provide social services oblivious of the economic consequences of what it is doing. Simply because the markets of the world have been swept up into a world market whose mechanisms are far beyond the reach of those who manage religious institutions, and whose complexities escape the tools of ordinary moral theology, does not justify ignorance of the problem when it comes to deciding about the protection and spread of existing organizations. If those committed to work at the frontiers of the Church, its missioners, can do no better than shrink their conscience to the size of laws that govern international economics, there is little hope of a graceful disestablishment of more centralized Church structures at odds with its own commitment to those victimized by the ruling economic order. In such matters, as Aloysius Pieris likes to say, the pastoral magisterium of the bishops and the academic magisterium of the theologians are meaningless without the "third magisterium" of the poor.[14]

Happily, these are questions that the Christian mission need not face alone. The rising chorus of voices from the Buddhist world of southeast Asia, often facing strong opposition from institutional Buddhism, has opened the way to collaboration with like-minded Christians in rethinking the institutional presence of organized religion.[15] But there is little chance of opening Christianity's moral agenda to Buddhist reflection, and vice-versa, without a common commitment to what I have loosely called the spiritual sensitivities of the age. As difficult as this is for the mainline churches of the Christian West, the problems multiply in many of the countries of Asia, where not even pluralism and dissent *within* the Church have been an essential part of the Christian identity, and where the only contact tolerated with local religiosity has been at a purely formal level.[16] For the churches of Asia, the frontier of Christianity begins not in the encounter with Buddhism but a step further back: at the point of disassociating the Christian conscience from social convention and reconnecting it with the deeper rhythms of the national soul.

Efforts need to be made to relocate the center of Asian theology from its present position in Western seminaries to a more suitable climate closer to the native religiosity of Asian cultures.

The attempt to create an Asian theology by exiling Asian seminary students to the universities of the West, arming them with "universal" ideas and "neutral" methodologies, repatriating them in their homelands, and then setting them up as teachers of Christian thought are inherently self-defeating. The 200 million Christians of Asia already speak a borrowed language as it is. To single out promising young minds from their midst for study abroad and discipline them to theological models, up-to-date though they be by foreign standards, only adds insult to injury. By the same token, to inflict the curricula of Europe on theological schools of Asia to the neglect of the rich mine of religious resources at hand, and then to ask them to adjust what they have learned to their own culture, is to trivialize the entire theological enterprise itself.

Needless to say, the solution is not to isolate Asian Christianity from all financial and educational contact with the churches of Europe and the United States. Indeed, experience shows that missionaries trained locally with only their own resources risk slipping from an anti-Western stance into a nationalistic one, which translates into foreign mission endeavors every bit as colonial as what they were rejecting. It comes as no surprise that breakaway forms of Christianity also end up isolating themselves from the universality they set out to enlarge.[17]

Looking around at what has happened with the confluence of the modern nation-state, nuclear arsenals, and global finance, the Christian mission can no longer boast, "The world is our parish." The parochialization of cultures as offspring of a single Mother Church—call it the body of Christ or call it the new global order—is no longer acceptable, and the theological tradition that supported it is in need of a radical plurality it has not yet achieved. The mainline churches have time and again shown themselves recalcitrant to reform in this area, with the result that many of the most creative minds in Asian theology waste their time rattling the chains of captivity in the academic press rather than get down to the work of doing theology with Asian resources. The clamor for attention is as deafening as the missionary response has been mute.

Resources will have to be invested in the creation of alternative forms of family living, particularly in urban centers.

As we watch Christianity's churches and cathedrals turned into museums, its seminaries sold off to be used for everything from prisons to think-tanks, and its monasteries and religious houses emptying out into apartment blocks, it is hard not to admit that something dramatic has happened to the "Christian community." It is not just that Church finances have fallen on hard times or that its architecture no longer expresses or enhances the values that bind the faithful together.

The closer one gets to the heartbeat of civilization in the modern megalopolis, the more it becomes apparent that the very basic structures of society on which the Christian community relied have collapsed and the pieces strung back together in loose and provisional alliances, contracted to suit the mobility of the modern ethic of work and entertainment. To those living in the urban environment, which is a growing majority of the planet, the term *family* no longer connotes its dictionary sense of a common household sharing a common life under one roof. The mission corps of the churches seems by and large to have accepted these circumstances as symptomatic of some deeper malady which is best addressed by working for change within the limits imposed by normal urban life.

For the more adventurous, this means identifying with the conditions of the inner-city poor in order to work together for improving conditions. Successful challenges to the basic structures that affect both the haves and the have-nots, however, have been as abstract and ineffective after public commitments to the "fundamental option for the poor" as before.

It does not take much reflection to realize that siding with the poor cannot be translated simply into the option of living the way the poor do, both because the very fact of having the option is a luxury denied the poor, and because few poor in their right mind, given the choice, would opt for it. The challenge of the mission is to rethink wealth and sufficiency in the light of the symbols of the

Christian faith, to conceive of architecture convivial to that rethinking, and to construct models to bring the idea from utopia to the reality of the modern city.

Whatever version of a "simple life" supported by "good work" and "stable family relationships" is created, it is likely to require considerable financial resources to execute, resources that would have to be diverted from traditional service institutions. At present, only the super-rich can afford to live within bicycling distance of work, to eat fresh vegetables grown locally and free of chemicals, to wear clothes not imported from halfway around the world, and to participate daily in the education of the children in their household. There is no indication that current models of "urban development," whatever their motivations, even dream of making this a possibility for the ordinary citizen. One is hard put to imagine a more appropriate reinvestment of finances used to support the dying institutions of the Church's mission corps than on the vocation to create a simple, sustainable family life in the midst of the cities across the world. All that is wanting is the will and discipline to justify the shift.

As long as one's focus stays fixed on the foreground of Church agenda, much of this may seem impractical and precipitous. But if one pulls back and restores to view the wider background of a Christian consciousness slowly disassociating itself from Church affiliation, of an institutional Church in the process of shrinking to a fraction of its present strength and size, the possibilities no longer look so strained and unrealistic.

Let the functionaries of particular church institutions choose to greet as they may the prospects of the kairos that is casting its shadow over their day-to-day calendar. In the interim, the way the mission efforts are directed and the frontiers at which they are spent will have important consequences for those who choose to remain, seeking to cast bridges between those who find the way to Jesus in the Church and those who prefer discipleship extra ecclesiam.

While the leadership of mainline Christian churches continue to quibble over the depth of secular humanism and the correct diagnosis of the world's ills, new religious movements continue to flourish all around them. As we approach the year 2000, more and more of these movements take on apocalyptic traits and feed on millennial superstitions, which only heightens apprehensions within established Christianity about the consequences of its failure to speak to the age. I have suggested a coincidence—not a cause-and-effect relationship, but only a synchronicity—between the apocalyptic mood and the coming abatement of ecclesial Christianity.

I would like to conclude by considering for a moment what this coincidence might mean for those of us who have chosen to secure our religious identity to the Christian tradition.

There can be no doubt that religious movements identified with the turn to the third millennium will differ from the infamous but overrated "Terrors of the Year 1000." For one thing, obedient to the age, these movements will be secularized, feminized, science-fictionalized, technologized, and—at least in the United States—politically corrected. By any account, this will be the most carefully monitored religious transition in history.[18] Although its effects will probably blow over with no more lasting impact than that left ten centuries ago, many who live through the period are likely to be faced with serious religious choices they might otherwise have avoided.

Despite the continued spread of scientific culture and the sophistication of religious studies, there is nothing to suggest that twentieth-century millennialism will be any more rational in the years ahead than it has been in years past. In the Christian lands of Europe and the Americas, works of respectable religious and theological research are being thrown together on shorter and shorter shelves in the bookstores to make room for the explosion of popular material on esoterica, prophecy, cults, magic, and the like. Meantime, scholars stumble over one another to name the vacuum in the human spirit that this industry has rushed to fill: a self fragmented by too much mobility and too many roles, an anonymity imposed by a complex social order, a frustration with having to entrust more and more of the things of life to a priestly caste of experts, and of course a general weariness with the irrelevance of traditional religion.

Whatever the most plausible explanation (or explanations, since it is unlikely that any one theory can manage the variety), a common ingredient coincident with the implosion of overextended ecclesial institutions is the longing to "connect" in more tangible, understandable terms to an age of overconnectedness. We carry stamps on our identity cards indicating that our bodily parts are now part of an "open market" for distribution after death; in place of unifying ideas we are swept along by "news" and shuttled from one bit of information to the next before we can make up our minds on how to put it all together; our immediate circle of relations is swept up into this same internet of transience and disjointedness. The need is for reconnecting—*re-ligio*. So acute can this need become that even critical reason will be sacrificed to fill it. This is the point at which Christian faith must break camp, namely, the point where what we call *fundamentalism* begins.

"Fundamentalism of whatever tradition," writes David Tracy, "and by whatever criteria of truth one employs seems to me irretrievably false and illustory."[19] In matters of the spirit, I would add, it is also pathological. Simple religious illiteracy is something else, and it would be the height of arrogance, not to mention of historical ignorance, to pass a sweeping judgment against it. But the superimposition of a literal account of cosmic realities on religious symbolism, for whatever reason, is inimical to faith. When fixed to an institutional base and a concrete community of believers, and particularly when bound to religious illiteracy, this literalism draws strength from the noblest of religious and moral aspirations, obstructing the basic question it poses for religious consciousness. One must therefore always take care in a critique of fundamentalism that one's sights are set on the culprit and not its supporting cast.

The battle against millennial movements need not command any central position in the Church's mission. In any case, as I said at the outset, it is not the response of the organized religions that will be decisive in their disappearance. At the same time, faith in Christian values obliges the believer—whether in the Church, straddling its fringes, or standing outside—to a certain commitment to reasonableness that cannot be overridden by any commitment to scholarly objectivity or to the fate of particular Christian institutions. Christianity would gain nothing by forfeiting its critical spirit in order to welcome all secular spirituality and religious movements on a principle of pure tolerance. Granted the need for a certain "principle of parity" in religious studies,[20] this does not oblige a faith tradition to loosen its claim on truth until all the evidence is in—which of course it never is. A faith without decisiveness, a faith that does not cut itself off, would be careless. The decision that religious expression of eternal truths is radically plural, and that religious accounts of the facts of the cosmos are always corrigible has no choice but to view fundamentalism as a spiritual disease.

Nothing in the spirit of interreligious dialogue contradicts this position. Enhancing tolerance among religious groups living together is never served by closing an eye to elements of intolerance, however central to a particular faith these elements may appear to be. What does contradict the commitment to reasonable faith is the resurgence of fundamentalist tendencies within the mainline Christian churches themselves. Popular Christian spiritualities riding on the wave of renewed interest in immediate religious experience, and bolstered by vestiges of literalist dogmatics, slide perilously close to denial of faith's search for critical insight. No amount of spiritual experience can ever take the place that disciplined study and reflection plays in passing on a comprehensive vision of human life from generation to generation, which is precisely what the Church aims to do and why some of us continue to exercise our Christianity within the Church. But as the Church gets smaller and opposing sides are thrown into the same quarters with more and more regularity, confrontations over this question are likely to increase.

This may not, as I have said, mean very much to society at large, but it means everything for the Church. Today we see the central symbols of Christianity sinking roots in spiritualities across the world, perhaps in simpler and more naïve forms than theology can stomach, but digestible to the needs of the age. To distance oneself from the ecclesia, not just the hierarchical head-quarters but the ecclesia as such, no longer obliges one to distance oneself from Christianity or its universal mission. In such circum-stances, the role the Church will play in maintaining tradition remains as momentous as ever. Without a firm commitment to a self-critical account of its beliefs and symbols, there is no hope of the Church's participating in its own resurrection as a leaven in the wider Christianness of cultures. In that sense, the struggle against fundamentalism in all its forms may be more important for the churches than for the rescue of those swept up in the dark side of new religious movements.

The emergence and appeal of new religious movements raises one final question which is always lurking in the background. "How many centuries is it," asked André Malraux, "since a great religion shook the world? This is the first civilization capable of conquering the entire planet, but not of inventing its own temples or its own tombs"[21] As we stand in the final years of the twentieth century and strain to see clearly ahead, the possibility that a new religion might indeed rise up to conquer the world, overshadow-ing the world religions as we know them, no longer sounds as rhetorical as it once did. Twenty-five years ago John Dunne sug-gested that "maybe one is rising now out of the meeting and confluence of the religions of the past."[22] The grounds for opti-mism that a world religion will rise out of the disciplines of inter-religious dialogue and study have long since eroded. The momen-tum has shifted clearly in the direction of religious pluralism.[23]

It is no accident that the Christian churches have a greater interest in studying new religious movements than such movements have in studying institutional Christianity. The more civilized the Church becomes and the more open to the pluralism of other religious ways, the less likely it is to shake world history. The same can be said of the tender-minded universalist movements that freely welcome all other religions under a sprawling umbrella of eclectic teachings. But it is the fundamentalist, uncritical, uncivilized, commercially enterprising religions of the world that grow stronger as Christianity and Buddhism—and yes, even Islam—grow more docile. Such movements see dialogue and collaboration with other religious organizations as no more than a means to avoid persecution. And many of them harbor the dream, often explicit, of shaking world history free of its traditional religious attachments.

What time is it for Christianity? The same time it is for history: a time when new religions are coming to birth. If a new religion were to arise in our times and plant a seed in the world with the potential to inspire history and culture the way Christianity itself has, the institutional Church would not even recognize it, let alone condone it. On principle, it cannot.

But what of the faithful? Will not many, in fidelity to their beliefs, continue to act as if it Christianity were never to be superseded and at the same time remain open to the possibility that it might? The same critical spirit of faith-seeking-understanding that Christianity will need to survive the disestablishment of its present ecclesial form must also leave open the possibility of still more radical transformations of its faith. In the meantime, there is much to do and much to refrain from doing. Because we have understood the causes and limits of fundamentalism, we do not for that reason have to tolerate it; it needs to be changed. Because there is much in the spirituality of the millennium that we do not understand, we do not for that reason have to try to change it into something else; it needs to be let alone in the hopes that there is more to understand. On the temper and exercise of these three virtues—understanding, tolerance, and the will to change—the relation of Christian faith to the Church and to the saeculum hangs.

NOTES

[1] Jan Van Bragt, "Apocalyptic Thought in Christianity and Buddhism," *Inter-Religio* 31 (1997): 7.

[2] The passage from Marx bears repeating if only because it is so little known in full: "Religious suffering is at one and the same time the expression of real suffering and a protest against real suffering. Religion is the sigh of the oppressed creature, the heart of a heartless world and the soul of soulless conditions. It is the opium of the people." Karl Marx, *Early Writings* (New York: Vintage, 1975), 238.

[3] In Asia, the latest symbolic event is the excommunication of the theologian Tissa Balasuriya. According to his fellow Sri Lankan Aloysius Pieris, an appeal to the Vatican's highest court, the Apostolica Signatura, against the illegality of the act was duly accepted by the court as a valid case, but then set aside because the Pope is reported to have given his approval to excommunication promulgated by the Congregation for the Doctrine of the Faith which—Pieris reminds us not without a certain animus—is "the successor to the notorious Holy Office of the Inquisition." "The Mahāpurisa Ideal and the Principle of Dual Authority," *Dialogue* 23 (1996): 176. See also two books on the subject: Basil Fernando, *Power vs. Conscience: The Excommunication of Fr. Tissa Balasuriya* (Hong Kong: Asian Human Rights Commission, 1997); *Truth and the Ambivalence of Power: Documents Relating to the Excommunication of Tissa Balasuriya*, special edition of *Logos* 35, 2–3 (1997).

[4] I am not unaware of the growing dissent within the churches from the right, the emergence of various sorts of elite corps of conservationists within the churches, and the extra-ecclesial reconstructionist movements whose appeal leans heavily on a rejection of existing Christian institutions. The polarization is perhaps clearest in the United States. See, for example, Michael W. Cuneo, *The Smoke of Satan: Profiles of Right-Wing Dissent in Contemporary American Catholicism* (New York: Oxford University Press, 1997) and Pat Robertson, *The New World Order* (Word: Dallas, 1991). I consider these movements even more out of touch with what is happening to Christianity in our times than the mainline churches, and therefore more likely to lose membership to millennial movements than to counter them in any effective way.

[5] Recent data confirms the suspicion that only a small minority of those brought up in traditional Christian countries who convert to Buddhism see this as requiring a conversion away from Christianity to a "non-Christian" faith. A recent survey among women in France who had become Buddhist showed that only .8% of them recognized such a requirement. See Karl-Fritz Daiber, *Religion unter den Bedingunden der Moderne* (Marburg: Diagonal, 1995), 151.

⁶ In some cases, there is a direct correlation of disassociation, as data on near-death experiences (NDE) shows. An in depth-survey taken in Australia of fifty persons with NDE reveals that half of the sample (46%) claimed to have no religion at the time of their NDE (general population sample was 16%). Of these two-third had a religious upbringing but had abandoned religion prior to their NDE. Afterwards, 84% claimed to have no religion. Only 2 returned to religion—1 to Buddhism, 1 to Roman Catholicism. Both of them claimed that NDE had nothing to do with it. Attitudes to the value of organized religion and church attendance dropped markedly after the NDE. On the other hand, experiential attitudes to religion jumped dramatically: the importance of prayer, 48% to 74%; meditation, 12% to 60%; the quest for spiritual values, 20% to 88%; and guidance, 32% to 86%. See Cherie Sutherland, *Reborn in the Light* (New York: Bantam, 1992), 94–111. A much less rigorous, more impressionistic study, biased by a life-changing NDE of her own and discussions with others, concludes as follows:

> One-third of the people I interviewed continued in a traditional religious setting after their near-death experiences.... The remaining two-thirds, however, either cast aside religious affiliations or never had been involved in any to begin with. For these people, the spiritual path became paramount, as they shifted from standards and dogmas to a personal, intimate relationship with God. Surprisingly, the greater number came to join or support some type or organized, structured church or philosophy later on, some even originated churches of their own.

Phyliss Atwater, *Beyond the Light: What Isn't Being Said about Near-Death Experience* (New York: Birch Lane Press, 1994), 144.

⁷ J. Ratzinger, "Christian Faith and the Challenge of Cultures," *Origins* 24 (1995): 683–4. Emphasis added.

⁸ R. Panikkar, "Are the Words of Scripture Universal Religious Categories?", *Archivio de filosofia* 60/1–2 (1992): 383.

⁹ I have touched on this in a recent essay, "Thoughts against Catholicizing Health," prepared as part of an international project on medical ethics and critical care and reprinted in this collection.

¹⁰ An exhaustive essay by Georges De Schrijver, *The Paradigm Shift in Third World Theologies of Liberation: From Socio-economic Analysis to Cultural Analysis* (Leuven: Bibliotheek van de Faculteit Godgeleerheid, 1996), recounts the steps by which the positive encounter with the modern world which the Catholic Church embraced in Vatican II and Medellín has given way to a position of defensiveness and revisionism.

¹¹ In a colloquium held twenty years ago and published as *Toward Vatican III: The Work That Needs to be Done*, ed. by David Tracy with Hans Küng and Johann Metz (New York: Seabury, 1978), a major concern of many of the participants was

to safeguard the achievements of Vatican II against a central authority's attempts to undermine it. Today the agenda for a Vatican III would, alas, have to focus still more on that same concern.

[12] I have touched on these questions in an essay entitled "Christianity Today: The Transition to Disestablishment," included in the present volume.

[13] Time was when this was the judgment of mystics, visionaries, and a handful of farsighted theologians. This summer I discovered a book by Cardinal Josef Ratzinger, *Sal de la Tierra* (Madrid: Editorial Palabra, 1997), in which the head of the most powerful Vatican office acknowledges that the Catholic Church is in for still more dramatic reduction of its institutional presence throughout the world (pp. 18–19).

[14] Aloysius Pieris, "Interreligious Dialogue and Theology of Religions: An Asian Perspective," *Horizons* 20 (1993): 106–14.

[15] In this connection, see John D'Arcy May, "Development without Violence? Some Buddhist and Christian Sources for Development Ethics," *Seeds of Peace* 13/1 (1997): 18–25.

[16] In Japan, for instance, it was a deliberate policy from the time of the Meiji Restoration to restrict the importation of Christianity to one brand, namely that of the upper-class European, which focused on social institutions and education. Popular belief, the fat underbelly of Japanese culture, was viewed as superstitious and inferior, and as a result Christianity never quite managed to pry open the Japanese psyche and get inside.

[17] Throughout this century, Japan has seen numerous examples of indigenous Christian movements that have sidestepped Western Christianity in an attempt to remedy what they perceive as a form of colonization. Although some of them have enjoyed modest success, their failure to come to grips with the home countries of the Christian mission have left them for the most part unknown to Japanese Christian in the mainline churches. See Mark Mullins, "Christianity as a New Religion," in Paul Swanson et al., eds., *Religion and Society in Modern Japan* (Berkeley: Asian Humanities Press, 1993), 257–72, as well as his book-length study, *Christianity Made in Japan: A Study of Indigenous Movements* (Honolulu: University of Hawai'i Press, 1998).

[18] See the remarkable collection of essays edited by Thomas Robbins and Susan Palmer, *Millennium, Messiahs, and Mayhem: Contemporary Apocalyptic Movements* (London: Routledge, 1997).

[19] David Tracy, *Blessed Rage for Order: The New Pluralism in Theology* (New York: Crossroad, 1975), 135.

[20] See Jonathan Smith, *Drudgery Divine: On the Comparison of Early Christian-ities and the Religions of Late Antiquity* (Chicago: University of Chicago Press, 1990), 106.

[21] *Anti-Memoirs* (Hardmondsworth: Penguin, 1967), 11.

[22] *The Way of All the Earth* (New York: Macmillan, 1972), 24.

[23] One of the most convincing arguments I know for this shift can be found in Joseph S. O'Leary, *Religious Pluralism and Christian Truth* (Glasgow: Edinburgh University Press, 1996).